GALWAY CITY
THROUGH TIME
Brendan McGowan
& Tanya Williams

AMBERLEY PUBLISHING

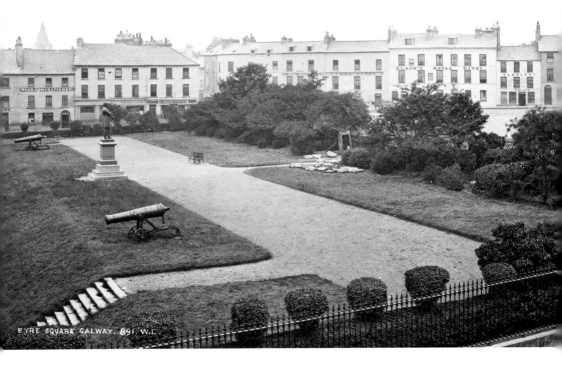

Eyre Square (North), *c.* **1905**
In the late nineteenth century the upper terrace of Eyre Square was adorned by a monument to Lord Dunkellin, unveiled in 1873, which was flanked by two Crimean Cannon, gifted to Galway in 1857. In 1905 an ancient doorway and first-floor oriel window, called the Borne Doorway, was re-built as the northern entrance to the railed square. Here it can be seen, in pieces, awaiting reconstruction.

First published 2013

Amberley Publishing
The Hill, Stroud, Gloucestershire, GL5 4EP
www.amberley-books.com

Copyright © Brendan McGowan & Tanya Williams, 2013

The right of Brendan McGowan & Tanya Williams to be identified as the Authors of this work has been asserted in accordance with the Copyrights, Designs and Patents Act 1988.

ISBN 978 1 4456 1763 3 (print)
ISBN 978 1 4456 1781 7 (ebook)

British Library Cataloguing in Publication Data.
A catalogue record for this book is available from the British Library.

Typesetting by Amberley Publishing.
Printed in Great Britain.

Introduction

Galway City lies at the mouth of the River Corrib, on the north-eastern shore of Galway Bay on the west coast of Ireland. The site of the present-day city has long been an important and strategic crossing point on the river, linking Lough Corrib to the Atlantic.

In 1124, Turlough O'Connor, King of Connacht and High King of Ireland, built a fortification in the vicinity called *Dún Bun na Gaillimhe*, 'the Fort of the Mouth of the River Gaillimh' (now the River Corrib). Following the Anglo-Norman incursion into Connacht in the early thirteenth century, the de Burghs established a settlement on the east bank of the river. By the early fourteenth century, a compact town was enclosed by a curtain wall and was beginning to flourish as a result of trade.

A charter granted by King Richard III in 1484 empowered Galwegians to elect their own mayor and bailiffs. It effectively released Galway from the grip of the de Burghs, and cleared the way for the rise to power of the 'Tribes of Galway'. A sustained period of prosperity followed under the leadership of these fourteen merchant families: Athy, Blake, Bodkin, Browne, D'Arcy, Deane, Ffont, Ffrench, Joyes, Kirwan, Lynch, Martin, Morris and Skerrett.

Political upheavals in England during the seventeenth century had disastrous consequences for Galway, the arrival of Cromwell's forces in 1651 heralding a long period of decline. In 1652, after a nine-month siege marked by famine and disease, the town finally surrendered. In 1691, during the Jacobite–Williamite War, the town capitulated to the forces of William of Orange.

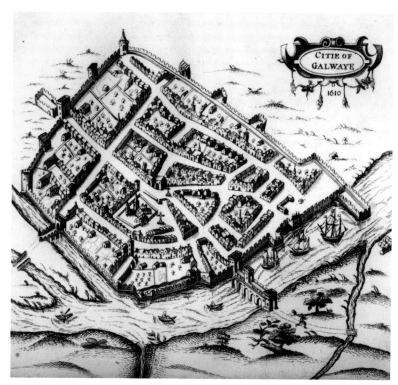

Citie of Galwaye
by John Speed,
1610.

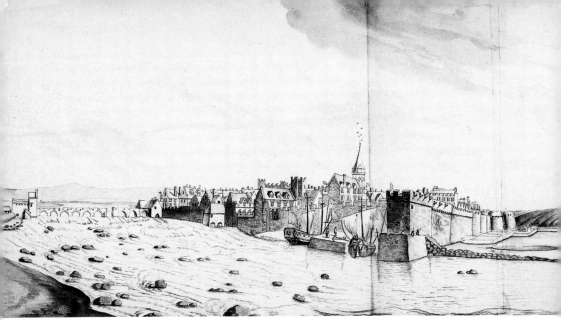

A Prospect of Gallway by Thomas Phillips, 1685.

There were signs of recovery in the early nineteenth century. A miniature industrial revolution, fuelled by the city's waterways, was taking place. Mills and warehouses sprang up in and around the town. New meat and fish markets were erected. Banks and hotels appeared around Eyre Square, which was railed and landscaped as a public park. A growing confidence and prosperity could be seen in its new buildings: Galway County Courthouse (1815), town and county gaols (1810), Gaol Bridge (1819) and church of St Nicholas (1821).

The Great Famine, however, dealt the city (and county) another blow, from which, it might be argued, it didn't fully recover until the latter twentieth century. Not even the opening of the Dublin–Galway line in 1851 and the completion of the Eglinton Canal the following year could halt the decline.

The fortunes of the city began to improve in the 1960s with the development of industry and tourism. Galway's first industrial estate opened in 1967 and a new Regional Technical College (now the Galway-Mayo Institute of Technology) was established in 1972. At the same time, the Irish tourism board, *Bord Fáilte Éireann*, was busy enhancing and promoting Salthill as the country's premier seaside resort. Galway City celebrated its 500th anniversary in 1984, and it was showing its age. Many areas within the city centre were in an abandoned and dilapidated state. These were designated a priority under the Urban Renewal Act in 1986 and by the early 1990s had been completely revamped.

Today, Galway is a modern and thriving city, and a centre of culture, learning and industry. Despite the dramatic changes that have taken place in recent decades, it has managed to retain much of its historic character.

This book, focusing on Galway's historic centre, the Claddagh, Salthill and the River Corrib, combines archive and contemporary images with informative captions to tell the story of this remarkable city and its people.

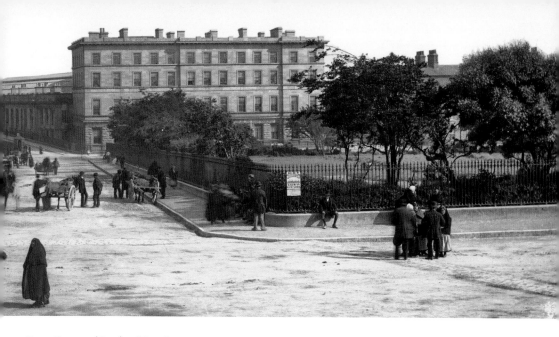

Eyre Square (East), 1880s & 1950s

On 12 May 1712, Edward Eyre, Mayor of Galway, gifted a plot of land outside the town's walls, east of its main gate, to Galway Corporation. In 1801, General Meyrick, sent to Ireland during the disturbances of 1798, had a square of 2 acres within the plot, enclosed with a low wall and laid out as a military parade ground. It was known as Meyrick Square before becoming Eyre Square.

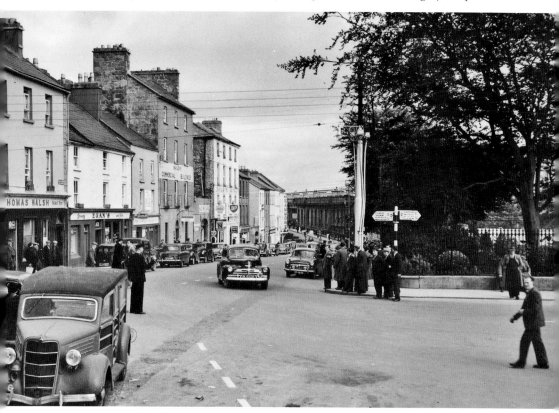

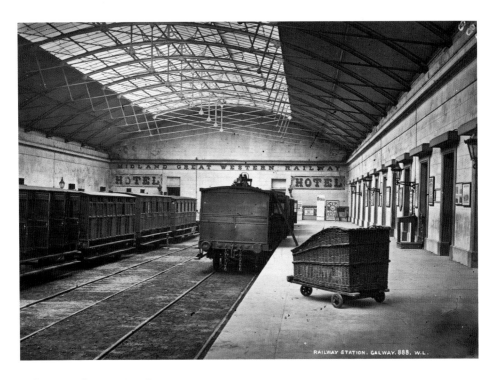

Galway Station, *c.* 1877 & 1950s
The Dublin to Galway line opened on 1 August 1851. Galway station was designed by
John Skipton Mulvany. Richard Turner, of Hammersmith Ironworks, Dublin, built the
25-metre-span roof over the station. It was the first design of its kind in Ireland and consisted
of curved beams covered with corrugated iron, and a considerable glass centrepiece. In 1966,
the 50th anniversary of the Easter Rising, the station was renamed Ceannt station in memory
of Éamonn Ceannt, the Galway-born signatory of the Proclamation of the Irish Republic.

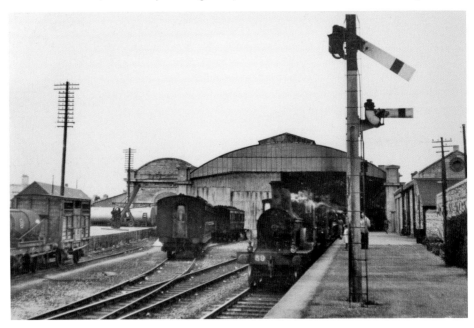

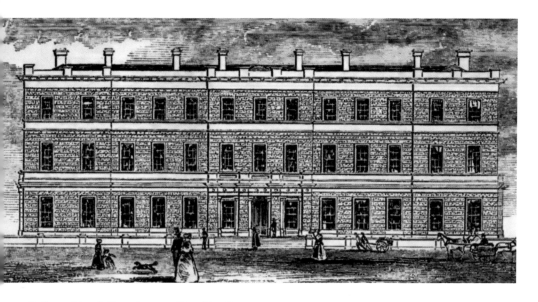

Railway Hotel, Eyre Square (South), 1854
The thirteen-bay, four-storey Midland Great Western Railway Hotel (later the Great Southern Hotel, and now the Meyrick Hotel) was formally opened in August 1852. It was hailed as 'the largest and most commodious provincial inn yet erected in the kingdom'. John Skipton Mulvany and William Dargan were responsible for the design and construction, which cost around £30,000.

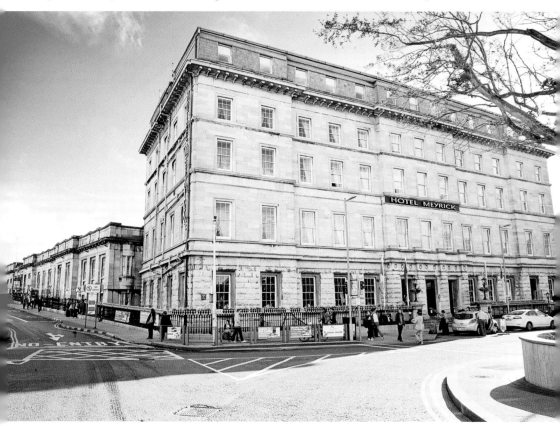

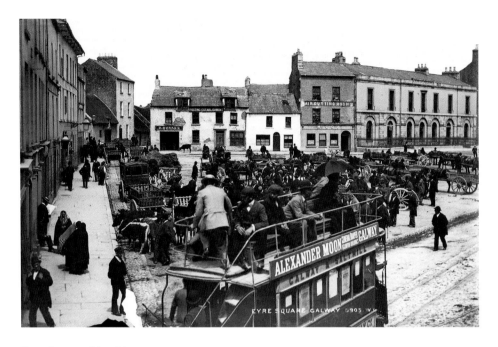

Eyre Square (North), *c.* 1900

In 1877, the Galway and Salthill Tramway Company was inaugurated, and two years later it opened a tramline linking its Forster Street depot, close to Galway station, to its terminus at Salthill. The tramline ran along the south and west of Eyre Square, before turning onto Williamsgate Street and continuing its journey to the seaside resort. The company eventually closed in 1919 as motorised transportation replaced horse-drawn transportation, and was succeeded by the Galway Omnibus Company. The building today, occupied by Dunnes Stores, was formerly James J. Ward's Motor Works, and before that the site was occupied by D. Burke's posting establishment.

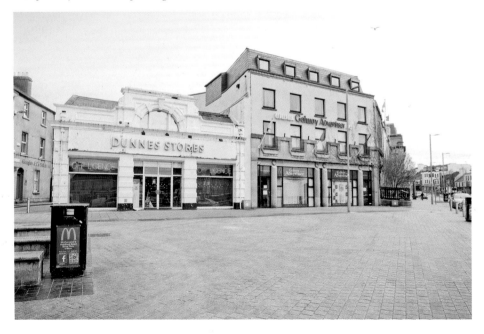

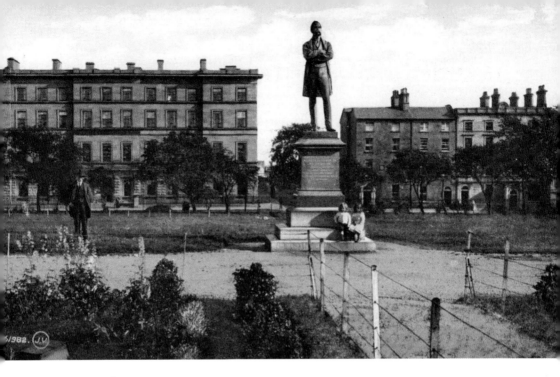

Dunkellin and Ó Conaire Monuments, Eyre Square, *c.* 1909 & *c.* 1940

In 1873 a memorial monument to Ulick Canning de Burgh, Lord Dunkellin, by the distinguished Anglo-Irish sculptor John Henry Foley (1818–74) was unveiled in Eyre Square. The inscription on the pedestal read: 'Lieu. Col. Lord Dunkellin, M.P., for the County of Galway. Born 1827. Died 1867. This statue was erected by the inhabitants of the County and Town of Galway as a tribute of affection and respect to his memory. 1873.' It was destroyed in 1922 as 'a symbol of landlord tyranny'. A monument to the Galway-born, Irish-language writer Pádraic Ó Conaire eventually took its place.

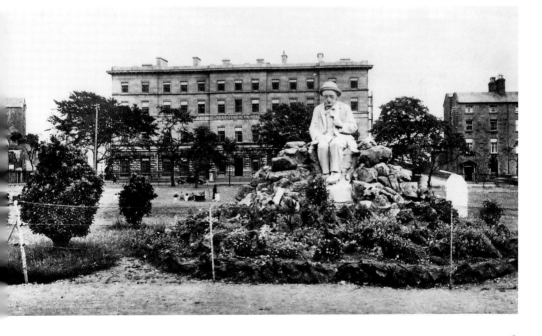

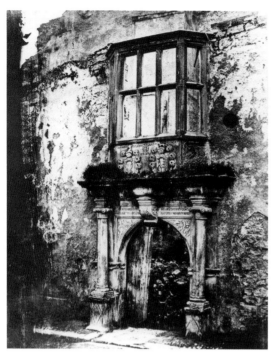

Browne Doorway, Abbeygate Street, 1880s

In the seventeenth century, Galway merchant Martin Browne and his wife Maria Lynch lived on Lower Abbeygate Street (then known as Skinner's Street). An arched doorway and first-floor oriel window fronted their house. Beneath the window, an armorial stone dated 1627 bore the family arms of Browne and Lynch, both belonging to the Tribes of Galway. In 1905, following proposals from the Galway Archaeological and Historical Society, Galway Urban District Council and County Council erected the Browne Doorway as the northern entrance to a railed Eyre Square.

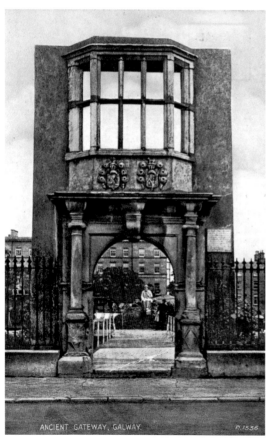

ANCIENT GATEWAY, GALWAY.

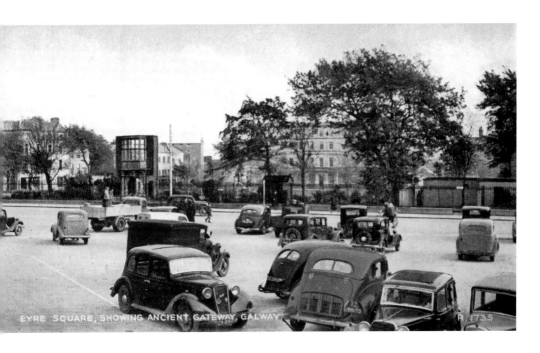

EYRE SQUARE, SHOWING ANCIENT GATEWAY, GALWAY. R.1735

Browne Doorway, Eyre Square, 1940s

Since the railings were removed from Eyre Square in 1964, the Browne Doorway has stood as a lone sentinel. It was due to be relocated to Galway City Museum but *An Bord Pleanála* (the Planning Board) ruled in 2002 that the 'Browne's Doorway shall be retained in its current location in the Square or relocated within the Square' because 'it is considered that the removal of the Doorway would be injurious to the cultural heritage of the Square'. Since then, a transparent protective case has been erected around the doorway.

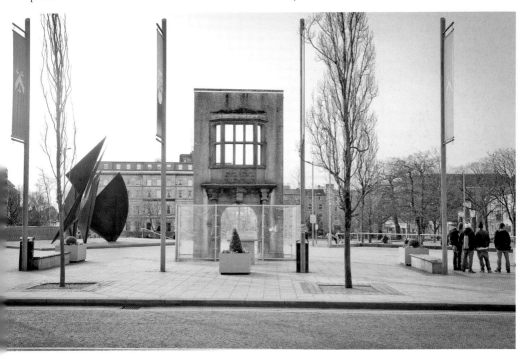

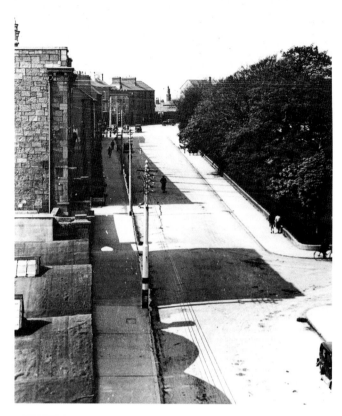

Eyre Square (West), 1940
This street was once immediately outside Galway's east-facing wall, which contained the main entrance to the medieval town. In front of the main gate, called the Great Gate and later Williamsgate, an open space was maintained. It was a defensive feature providing those defending the town with a 'field of fire'. This green is now known as Eyre Square.

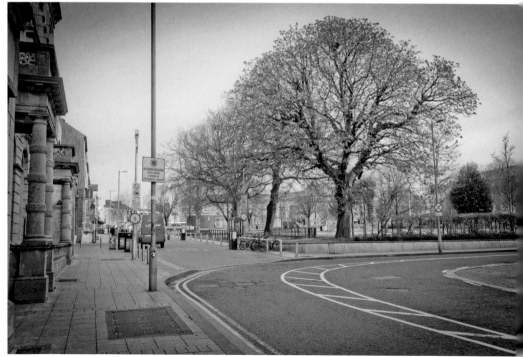

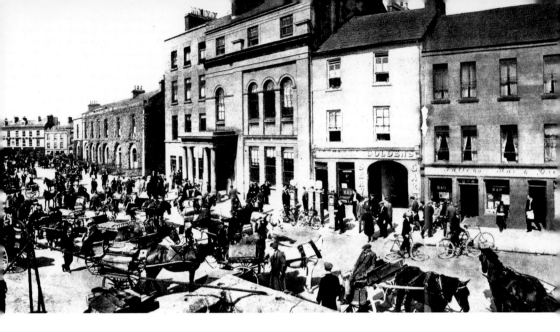

Eyre Square (North), 1945

This 1945 scene shows a busy Eyre Square during the Galway Races with horse-drawn carts and carriages waiting to take punters to Ballybrit Racecourse. The first race meeting at Ballybrit, on the outskirts of Galway, took place on 17 August 1869. According to contemporary accounts, the two-day event, advertised as 'Galway Races and Steeplechases', attracted 75,000 people. The main race was won by a horse named Absentee and was ridden by jockey W. Bell. The large building (centre) with the four-column portico was once Galway County Club where the landed elite met to discuss issues of mutual importance.

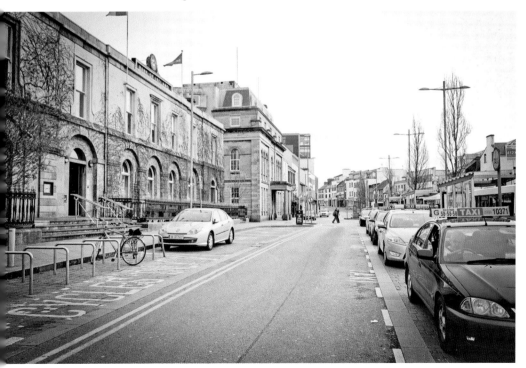

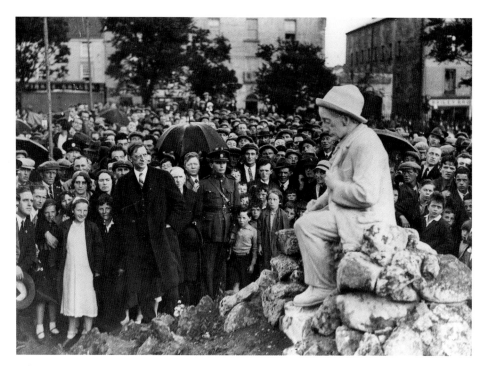

Ó Conaire Monument, Eyre Square, 1935

In 1928, the Galway-born, Irish-language writer Pádraic Ó Conaire died in the pauper's ward of Richmond Hospital, Dublin. His friends in the Galway Branch of the Gaelic League raised funds to erect a memorial in his honour and recruited the services of master sculptor Albert Power (1881–1945). In June 1935, the monument was unveiled by Éamon de Valera, then President of the Executive Council of the Irish Free State. In 2006, following several acts of vandalism, the statue was relocated to Galway City Museum for safekeeping.

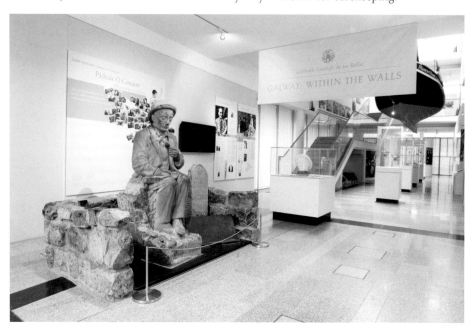

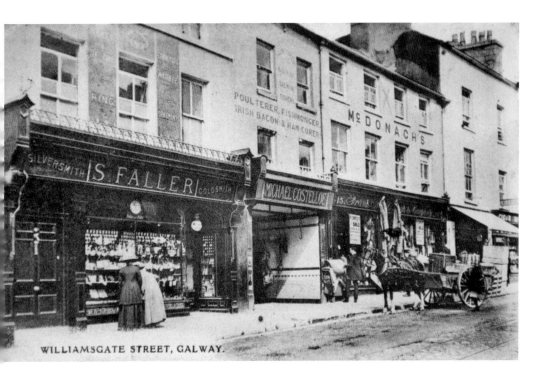

WILLIAMSGATE STREET, GALWAY.

Williamsgate Street, 1900s
As with William Street, Williamsgate Street is named in honour of King William of Orange, whose forces successfully laid siege to the town during the Jacobite–Williamite War (1688–91). Subsequently, the main entrance to the walled town of Galway, the Great Gate, was replaced by a newer gate, which became known as Williamsgate. In 1899 Faller's Jeweller's, established on Dominick Street in 1879 by Stephen Faller, moved to Williamsgate Street.

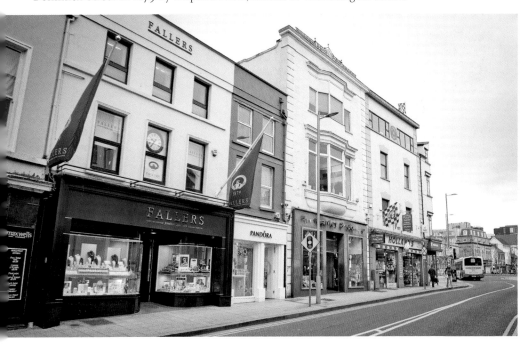

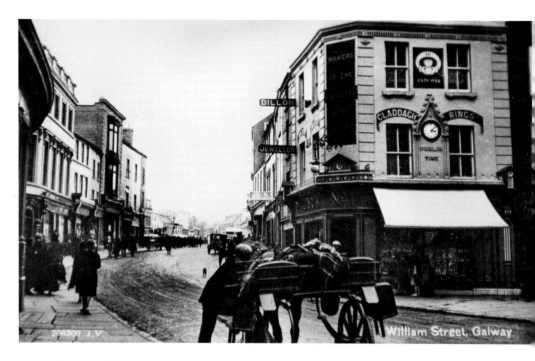

Dillon's, William Street, 1920s
The clock on the wall of Dillon's Jeweller's has shown 'Dublin time' for more than a century. In the past, Galway, like other Irish towns, operated according to local time, which was relative to its distance from Greenwich. Dublin time was twenty-five minutes behind London, and Galway time was eleven and a half minutes behind Dublin. With the arrival of the railways, this became problematic for timetables as the local time at one end of the line could differ significantly from that at the other. As Irish trains operated to time in the metropolis – Dublin time – Galway had to conform.

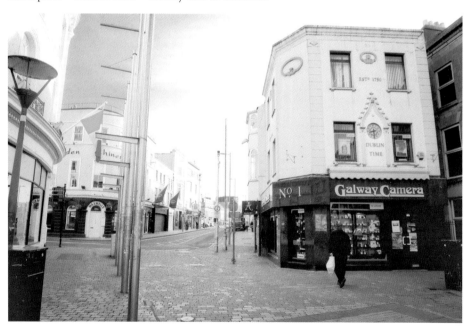

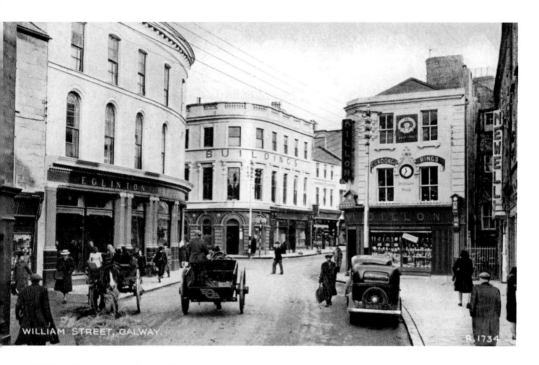

William Street & Eglinton Street, 1940s

On the junction of William Street and Eglinton Street are two curving buildings known as the Eglinton and the Colonial. They were designed in the 1860s by architect Edward Henry Carson, father of the Ulster Unionist politician Edward Carson whose statue looms over Stormont, Belfast. The Eglinton building is better known to Galwegians as Moon's after Alexander Moon's department store, which now trades as Brown Thomas. In the 1920s, Moon's was the official robe maker to the university in Galway. On the opposite corner, the Colonial building is better known locally as McNamara's.

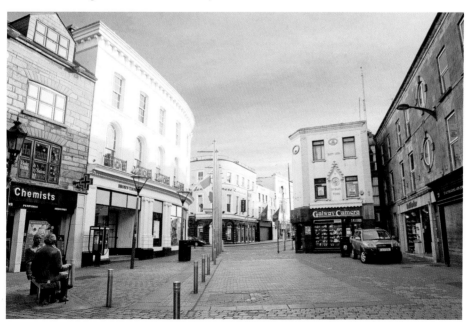

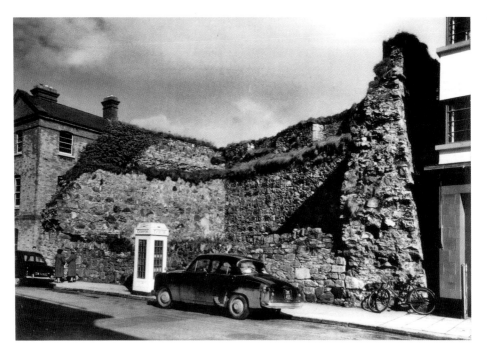

Lion's Tower Bastion, Eglinton Street, 1950s
In 1646, during the Irish Confederate Wars, a bastion was built around the Lion's Tower (erected in 1278) to strengthen the town's defences. When this photograph was taken the bastion lay in ruins. To its left is the large, red-brick *Garda Síochána* Barracks, formerly belonging to the Royal Irish Constabulary, and to the right is the Savoy Cinema. In the early 1960s Galway historian G. A. Hayes-McCoy led an ultimately unsuccessful campaign to preserve the landmark. An armorial panel bearing the arms of Galway, salvaged from the bastion, is incorporated into the present building.

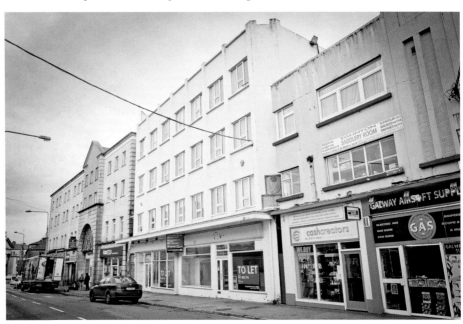

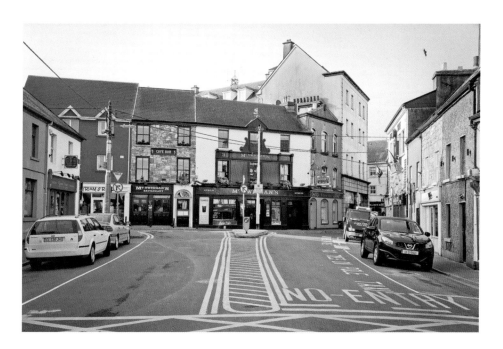

Flynn's Grocer's, Eyre Street, Woodquay, 1980s

In the nineteenth century a section of the River Corrib flowed through the heart of Woodquay as far as Eyre Street (where McSwiggans is today). Woodquay in Irish is *Barr an Chalaigh* meaning 'Upper Port'. It was the secondary port for the town, for inland trade using Lough Corrib. Before the construction of the Eglinton Canal, goods landed at the town's quays had to be transported the short distance to Woodquay by land before being shipped upriver. In 1986, Fylnn's bar and grocer's was replaced by McSwiggans bar.

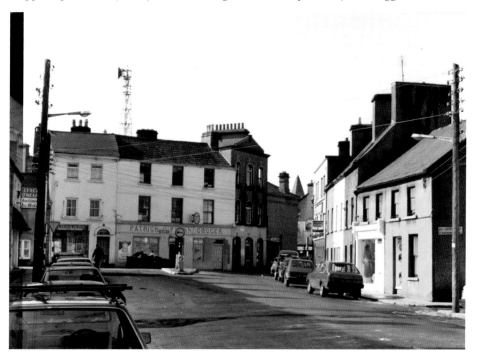

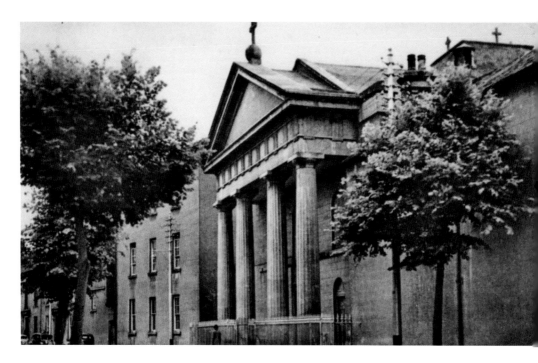

Abbey Church, Francis Street, 1940s

In the early nineteenth century, before Eglinton Street was constructed, St Francis Street was known as Woodquay Street. The Franciscan abbey church, founded in 1781, was remodelled in the late 1840s by architect James Cusack. From 1816 onwards, Cusack was very active in Galway, designing the pro-cathedral of St Nicholas (1816–21), the Bank of Ireland (1831) and the Presbyterian church (1833–35) at Nun's Island. The abbey church was finally consecrated in 1849.

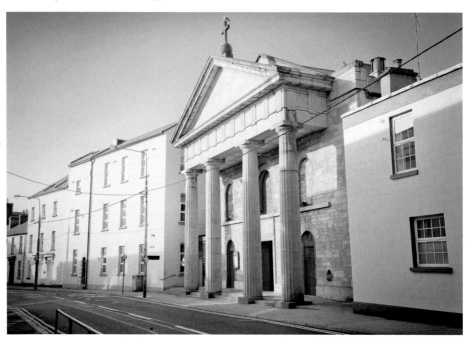

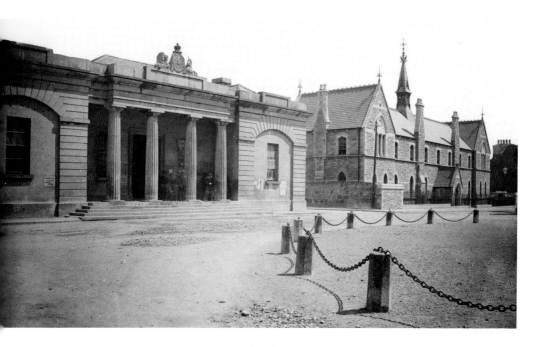

Town Courthouse and Sisters of Mercy School, Newtownsmith, *c.* 1900

In 1824 the town courthouse (*left*) was built at Newtownsmith directly opposite the county courthouse. The building cost £3,000 to construct and its design echoed that of its neighbour, though on a lesser scale. From the outset it served as both a courthouse and a town hall. By 1885 it had ceased to serve as a courthouse so, at the request of the town commissioners, it was converted into a town hall proper. The Gothic building seen here is the Sisters of Mercy school, opened in 1875, which has since been replaced by *Scoil an Linbh Íosa*, the Mercy primary school that opened in January 1960.

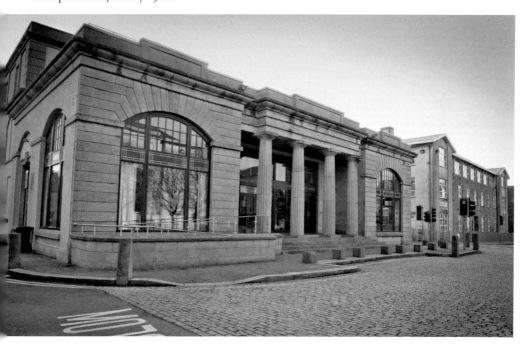

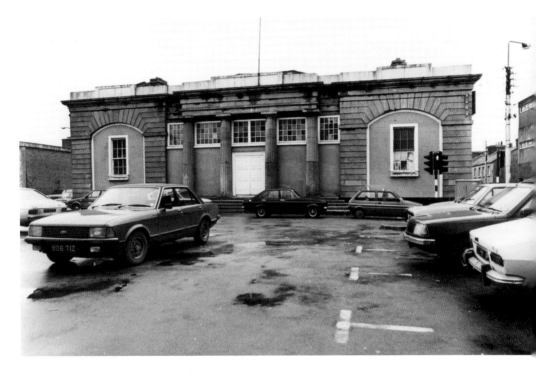

Town Hall Cinema, Newtownsmith, *c.* 1975

For much of the twentieth century the old town courthouse was the Town Hall Cinema. On 15 July 1921, notice of the Anglo—Irish truce that ended the War of Independence (1919–1921) appeared on its cinema screen. By the early 1990s the building had fallen into disrepair. Galway Corporation (now Galway City Council), with financial assistance from the Department of Arts, Culture and the Gaeltacht, refurbished the building which reopened as the Town Hall Theatre in October 1995.

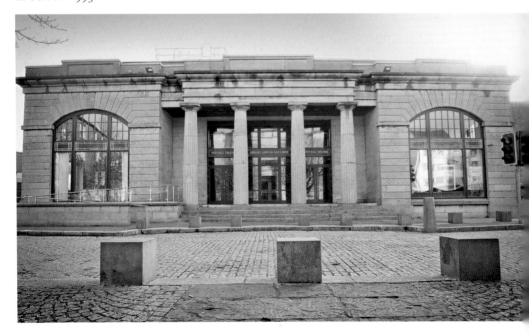

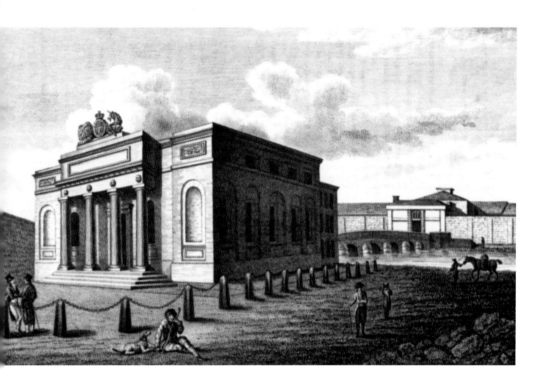

Galway County Courthouse, Newtownsmith , c. 1820

The county courthouse was erected between 1812 and 1815 and was linked to Galway County Gaol by Gaol Bridge, built in 1819. In 1820, Galway historian James Hardiman wrote that the court's 'lofty portico, entrance, and extensive hall [...] will immediately attract attention. It is altogether an edifice highly creditable to the county, and considerably ornamental to the town'. Today, the same building still serves as Galway's courthouse. The Cathedral of Our Lady Assumed into Heaven and St Nicholas, or Galway Cathedral, stands on the site formerly occupied by Galway County Gaol.

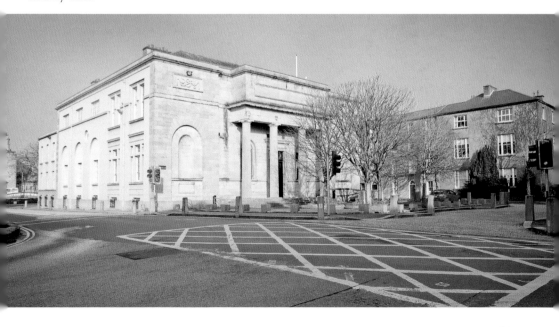

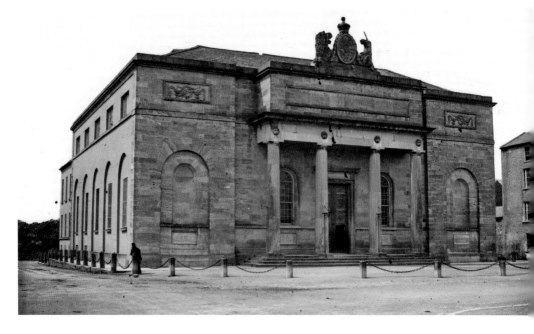

Galway County Courthouse, Newtownsmith, *c.* 1875

Galway County Courthouse was once adorned with the Royal Arms of George III (reigned 1760–1820), which comprised the arms of England, Scotland and Ireland, with a small central shield bearing the arms of Hanover, surmounted by a Royal Crown. The arms were flanked by a lion symbolising England and a unicorn representing Scotland (interestingly, it is depicted collared and chained). Following Irish independence, the Royal Arms were removed from the courthouse and now repose behind the 'Quad' in the grounds of National University of Ireland, Galway.

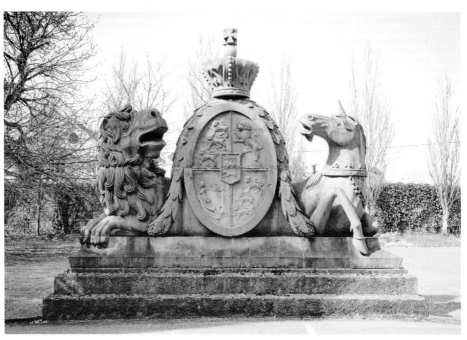

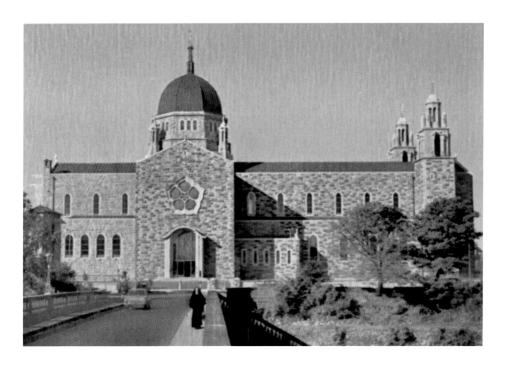

Galway Cathedral, Nun's Island, *c.* 1970

Dedicated by Cardinal Cushing of Boston in August 1965, the Cathedral of Our Lady Assumed into Heaven and St Nicholas, or Galway Cathedral, is one of the youngest of Europe's great stone cathedrals. Situated by the River Corrib, on the site of the former Galway County Gaol, its large green dome has for half a century dominated the Galway skyline. Inside, an eye-catching mosaic features an unusual alliance: Jesus Christ, Patrick Pearse and John F. Kennedy.

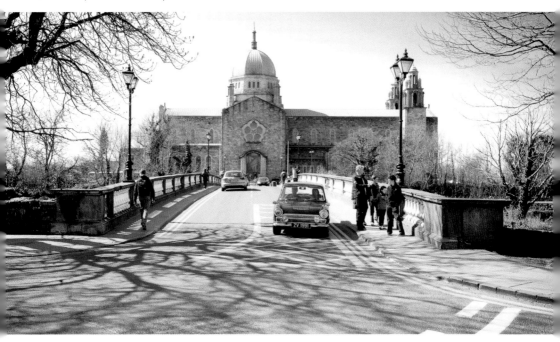

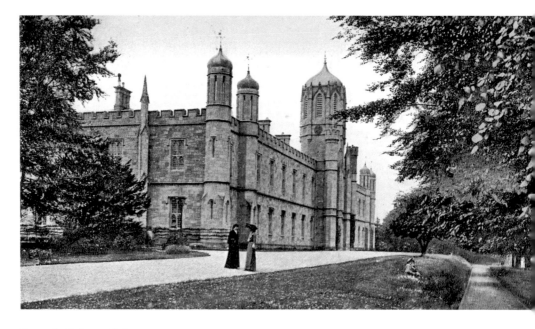

Queen's College, Galway, *c.* 1900

In 1845 British Prime Minister Robert Peel passed an act providing for the establishment of three Queen's colleges (at Belfast, Cork and Galway), 'in order to supply the want which had long been felt in Ireland for an improved academical education, equally accessible to all classes of the community without religious distinction'. In 1849 the non-denominational or 'Godless' colleges opened for teaching and the following year became the Queen's Universities of Ireland. In 1908 the Galway branch was renamed University College, Galway (UCG), and in 1997 it became National University of Ireland, Galway (NUIG).

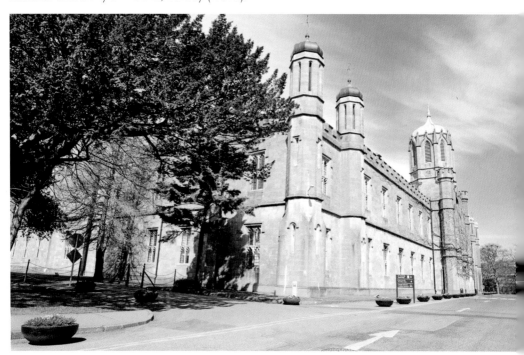

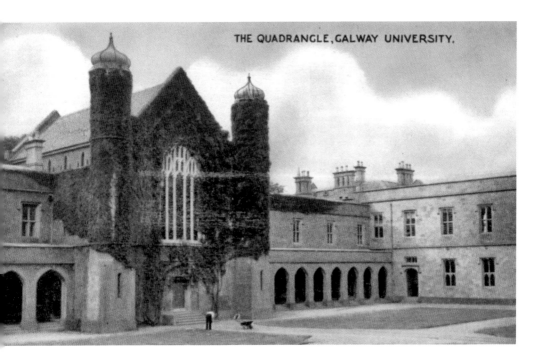

The Quadrangle, Galway University, *c.* 1900

Known as the 'Quad', the original quadrangle of Queen's College, Galway, was designed in 1845 by Dublin-based architect John Benjamin Keane. Of the three Queen's Colleges established in the 1840s only Galway was built with an enclosed quadrangle. It is built of local limestone in a Tudor-Gothic architectural style and is loosely modelled on Christ Church College at the University of Oxford. Today, it is mainly used for administrative purposes and houses the offices of the president and the vice presidents.

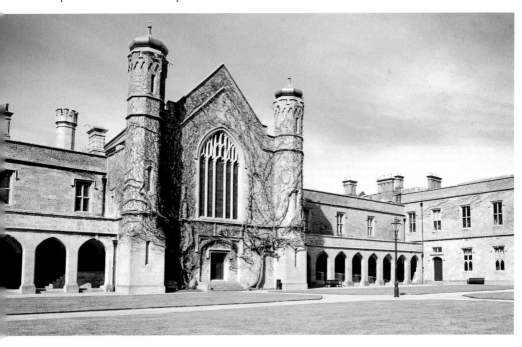

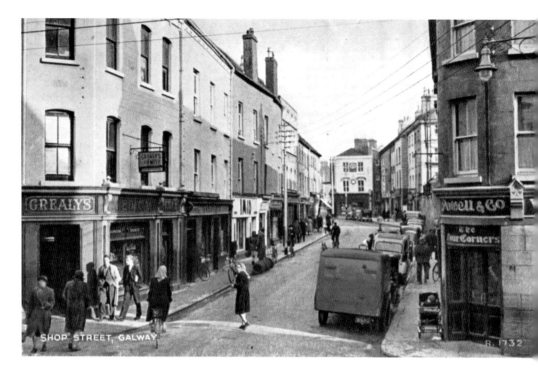

The Four Corners, 1940s

Na Ceithre Coirnéal, or the Four Corners, is the intersection of Shop Street, William Street, Upper Abbeygate Street and Lower Abbeygate Street. Lynch's Castle, built around 1500, dominates this important junction in the heart of the medieval town. On the opposing corner, Powell's music and stationary shop has been trading since 1918. Since the late 1990s these streets have been pedestrianised; however, delivery and street cleaning traffic is allowed each morning.

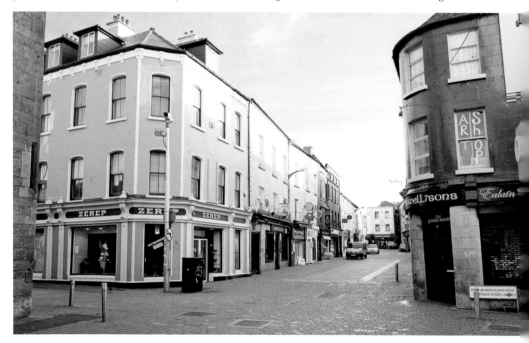

Lynch's Castle, Shop Street, c. 1820
The 'Tribes of Galway' was a term coined by Cromwellian soldiers to refer to the fourteen merchant families who effectively ran and controlled the medieval town. These tribes were, by name: Athy, Blake, Bodkin, Browne, D'Arcy, Deane, Ffont, Ffrench, Joyes, Kirwan, Lynch, Martin, Morris and Skerrett. Of the fourteen, the 'proud' Lynches were perhaps the most powerful, supplying the town with eighty-four mayors between 1484 and 1654.

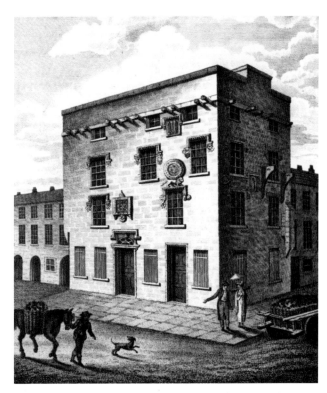

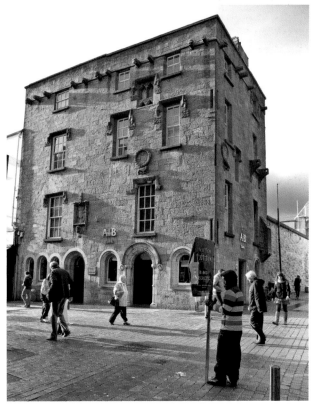

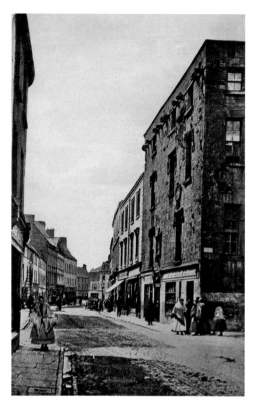

Lynch's Castle, Shop Street, *c.* 1900
Situated on the corner of Shop Street and
Upper Abbeygate Street, Lynch's Castle is
believed to have been built around 1500 as
evidenced by a stone panel displaying the
arms of Henry VII who reigned as King of
England and Lord of Ireland from 1485 to
1509. The castle was inhabited by the Lynch
family until 1654 when Thomas Lynch Fitz
Ambrose, Mayor of Galway, was expelled from
his ancient family seat by Cromwellian forces.
The castle has served as a bank since 1918.

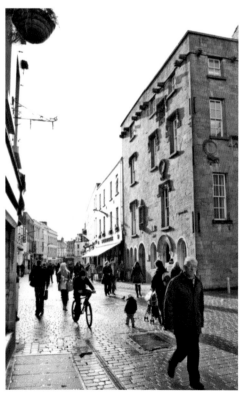

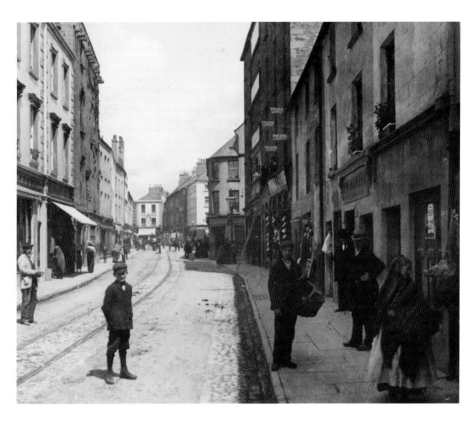

Shop Street, *c.* 1903

In the seventeenth century, Shop Street, which extends from the intersection of High Street and Mainguard Street to the Four Corners, was known as High Middle Street. Its modern name dates from the mid-eighteenth century and derives from the fact that Galway's first shops opened here.

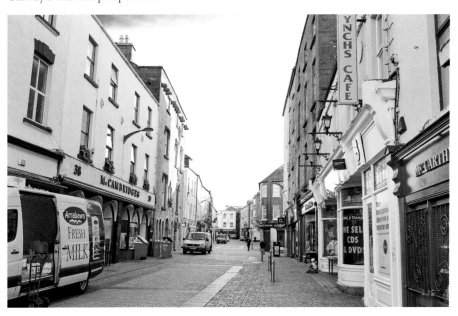

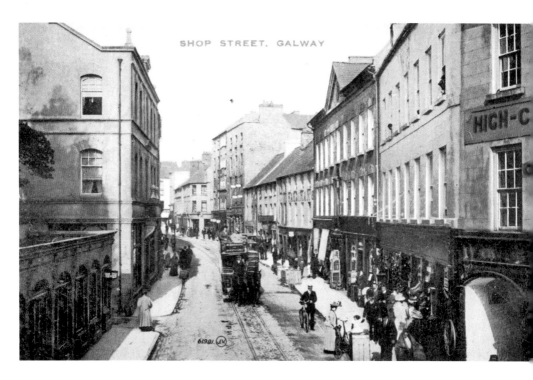

Shop Street, *c.* 1909 & 1940s

In the decades that separate these colour-tinted postcards of Shop Street, motorised transport has begun to replace horse-drawn transport and bicycles on the street of Galway but the streetscape is much the same. Anthony Ryan's draper's, seen on the right, was established in 1909 and is still thriving today.

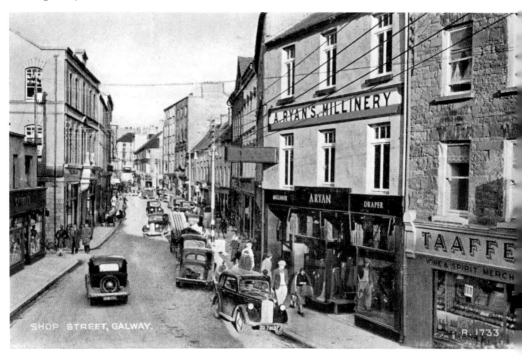

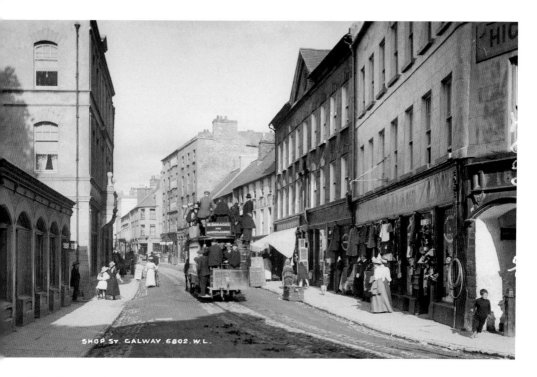

Shop Street, 1900s

Eason's three-story building on the corner of Shop Street and Church Lane was formerly O'Gorman's Bookshop and Printing Works. The business moved to No. 33 Shop Street in the early 1900s, and it was there that the *Galway Advertiser* newspaper was established in 1970. The printworks closed in 1986, followed by the bookshop three years later. Eason's opened in 1989.

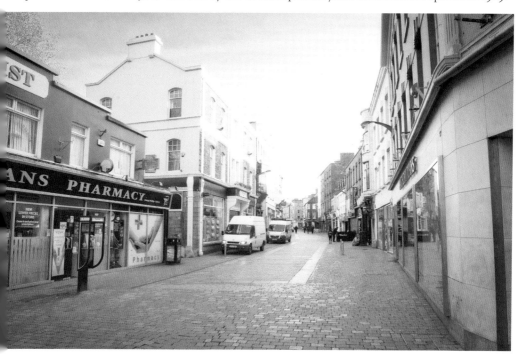

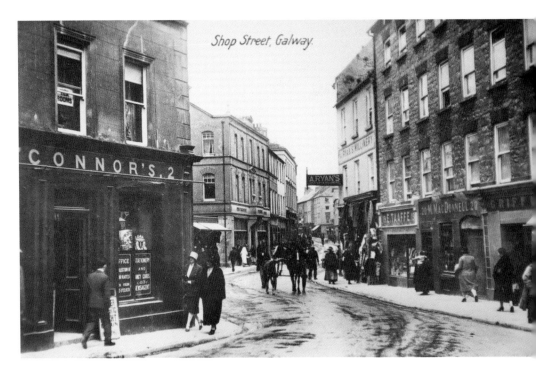

Shop Street, 1930s

In recent years many international chains – McDonald's, Boots, Schuh, Tommy Hilfiger and River Island – have opened along Shop Street. However, many long-standing Galway stores have held their own alongside these superstores, such as Ryan's Drapery, Taaffe's Bar and Griffin's Bakery.

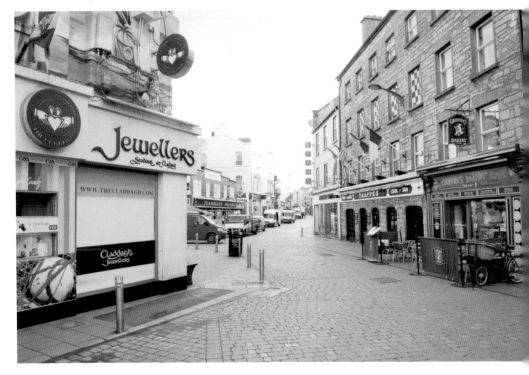

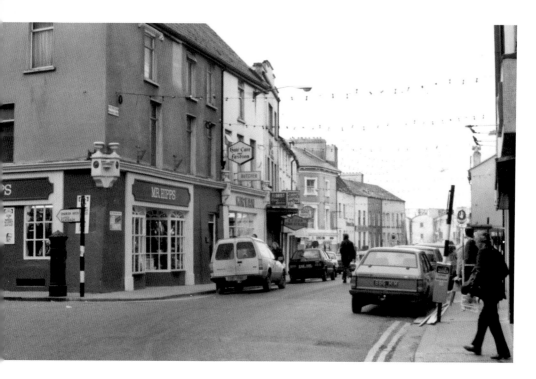

Mainguard Street, 1980s

There were two large barracks erected in Galway in the early eighteenth century. The Shambles Barracks at the end of Mainguard Street was erected in 1749 for ten companies of soldiers. Today, St Patrick's National School, opened in 1954, occupies the site. At the other end of the town was the Castle Barracks, built in 1734 for three companies of men. This barracks was demolished in the 1980s. The buildings forming the corner of Mainguard Street and High Street date to the seventeenth century.

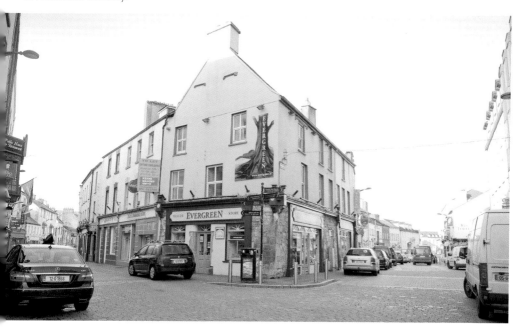

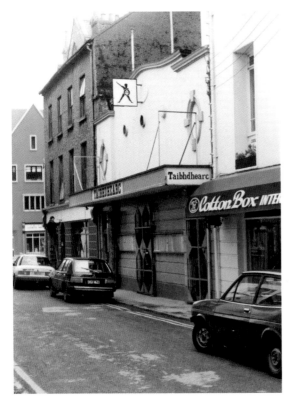

An Taibhdhearc, Middle Street, 1980s
Founded in 1928, *An Taibhdhearc* is the national Irish language theatre (*Amharclann Náisúnta na Gaeilge*). It is the oldest theatre still operating in Galway and the only theatre in Ireland devoted entirely to Irish-language productions. The name of the theatre was carefully chosen as the *Book of Armagh*, an early ninth-century manuscript, in which the Latin word *theatrum* was translated as *taibdercc* (modernised as *taibhdhearc*) – a combination of two Irish words: *taibhse* meaning 'spectacle' or 'ghost' and *dearc* meaning 'behold' (behold the spectacle!). In 2007 the theatre closed as a result of fire damage, reopening in 2012.

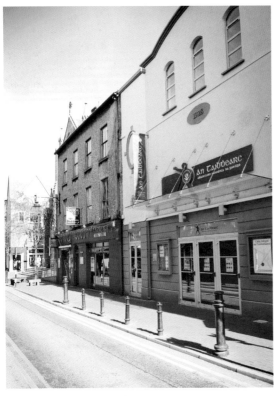

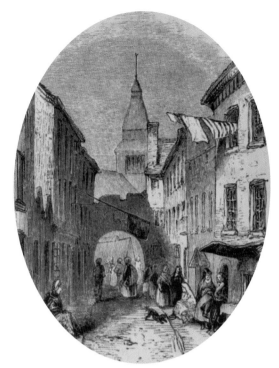

Buttermilk Lane, 1843
According to tradition, medieval Galway contained fourteen towers, fourteen streets and fourteen lanes, not to mention its fourteen Tribes. In the mid-seventeenth century Buttermilk Lane, which today connects Shop Street and Middle Street, was known as Lower Shoemaker's Lane. This print from a wood engraving is based on a watercolour by Evans of Eton, who allowed himself considerable artistic licence when he painted his 1838 view.

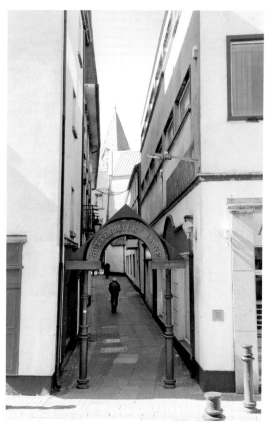

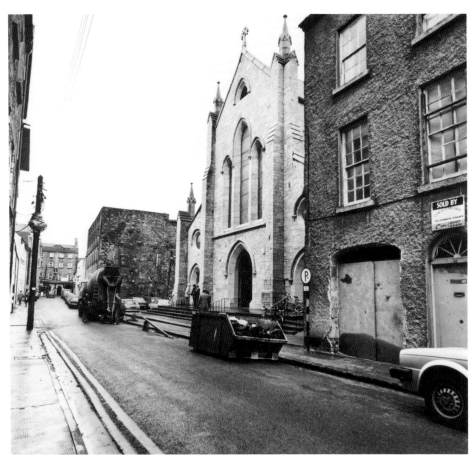

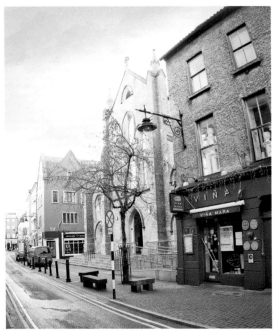

Church of St Augustine, Middle Street, *c.* 1975
Galway's original Augustinian friary was founded in 1508 and was located outside the town's walls on the site now occupied by Forthill Cemetery. Galway historian James Hardiman laid the foundation stone for the church of St Augustine at Middle Street on 28 August 1855. The building took four years to complete, formally opening on 4 September 1859. The church was completely renovated in the 1970s.

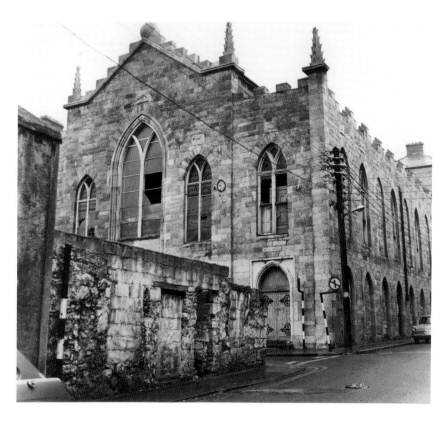

Church of St Nicholas, Middle Street, c. 1975
Designed by architect James Cusack, the parish church of St Nicholas was inaugurated in 1821. It became the pro-cathedral in 1831 on the establishment of the Catholic diocese of Galway. On Christmas morning 1842, during early morning Mass, the upstairs gallery collapsed killing thirty-seven people. The cathedral was closed in 1965 and converted for use as a commercial property.

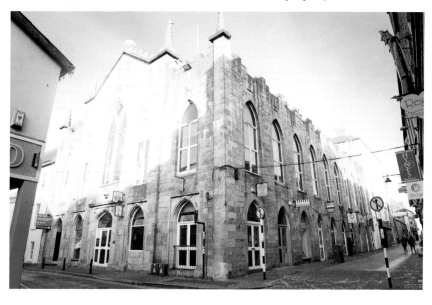

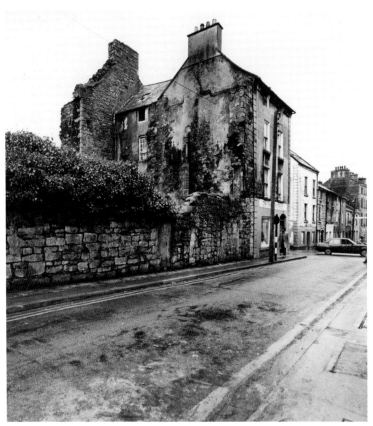

High Street and Quay Street, *c.* 1975

Linking Shop Street with Quay Street, High Street is so called because of its elevated or high position. In the 1980s this derelict corner of High Street and Lower Cross Street was demolished and rebuilt. Since then a number of new businesses have been enticed to this revamped part of town. In 1992, Dillon's Jeweller's, established in Galway in 1750 and formerly located on Williamsgate Street, relocated to Quay Street.

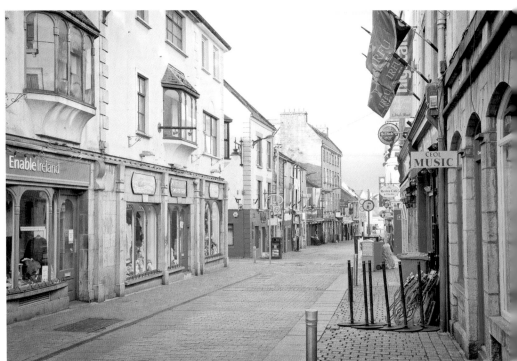

High Street and Quay Street,
c. 1950 & 1980s
Situated on the corner of Quay Street
and Upper Cross Street, Seaghan Ua
Neachtain's pub was established in 1894.
Known as *Tigh Neachtain* (meaning
'Naughton's House'), the building which
dates from the late sixteenth or early
seventeenth century has become an
iconic Galway landmark. In the
mid-1980s an ESB poll and its wires that
were obscuring the original first-floor
oriel window were removed, much to
the improvement of the area and the
delight of Galwegians.

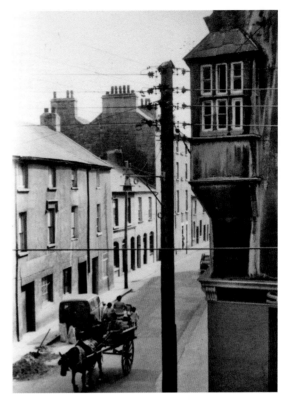

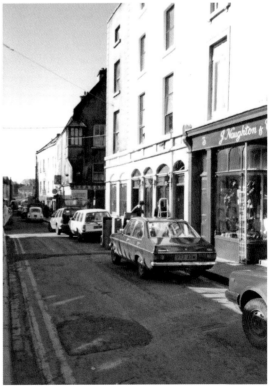

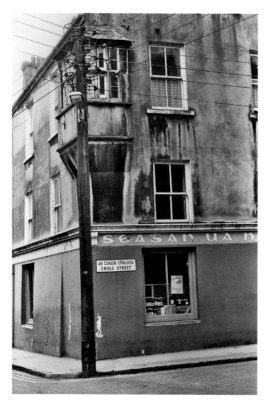

Tigh Neachtain, Quay Street, 1981
Tigh Neachtain was formerly the town house of Richard Martin (1754–1834), known as 'Trigger Martin' or 'Humanity Dick' for his reputations both as a duellist and as an animal rights activist. Born at Ballynahinch Castle, and raised upriver of Galway at Dangan House, Martin served as MP for Co. Galway at Westminster. He was the key figure behind the Cruel Treatment of Cattle Act 1822, sometimes referred to as Martin's Act. He was also present in 1824, when the Society for the Prevention of Cruelty to Animals (SPCA) was established in London.

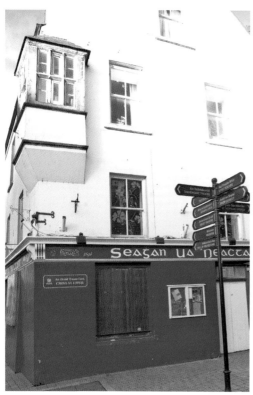

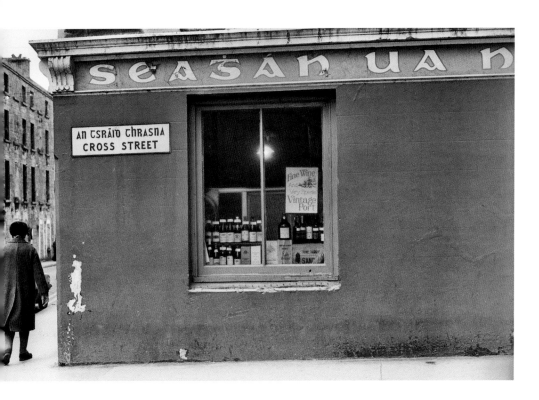

Tigh Neachtain, Quay Street, 1981

Richard Martin was a keen thespian and opened a theatre at Kirwan's Lane in 1783. On the opening night he and his wife, Elizabeth, shared the stage with a young actor named Theobald Wolfe Tone – 'the Father of Irish Republicanism' – who would go on to play a key role in the 1798 Rising. Martin leased this property close to the theatre so that he could entertain guests. In 1934, the bridge at the end of Quay Street was named Wolfe Tone Bridge.

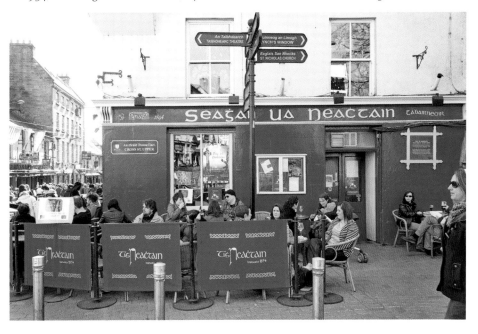

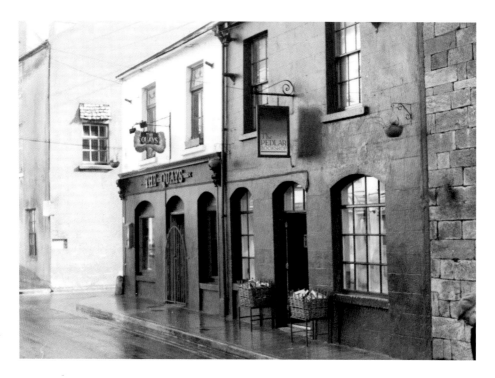

The Quays Bar, Quay Street, 1980s

Known as Kea Street (and later Watergate Street) this thoroughfare led to the medieval docks. The Quays bar was formerly Lydon's bar, a favourite haunt of local fishermen. The laneway beside the Quays, once called Red Earl's Lane, was later known as Courthouse Lane before becoming Druid Lane (after the Druid Theatre). The Pedlar Bookshop was formerly Ellwood's pawnshop. The wrought iron fittings which hold the bookshop's sign once held three brass balls, the symbol of the pawnbroker.

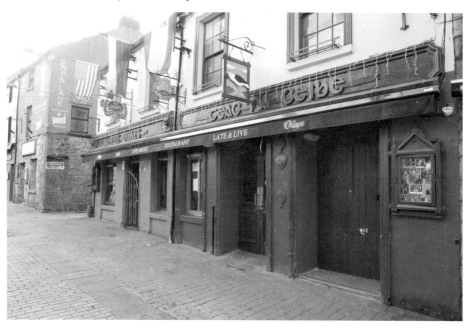

Kirwan's Lane, *c.* **1975**
Following the
Cromwellian conquest,
the protestant inhabitants
of Galway insisted that
the Mayor of Galway
be a Protestant and
an Englishman so, in
1654, Colonel Peter
Stubbers, who had led the
Cromwellian army into
Galway, was appointed
to the position. Kirwan's
Lane is named in honour
of John Kirwan
Fitz-Stephen who, in
1686, became the first
Catholic Mayor of Galway.
He held this title for
thirty-two years. By the
1980s, Kirwan's Lane was
derelict but was restored
to its former glory as the
result of urban renewal
tax incentives.

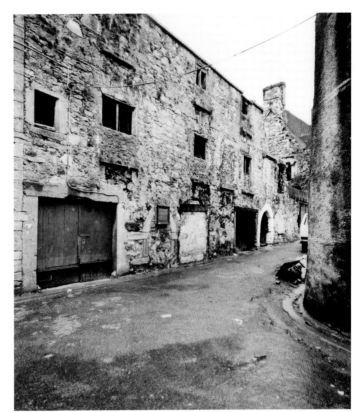

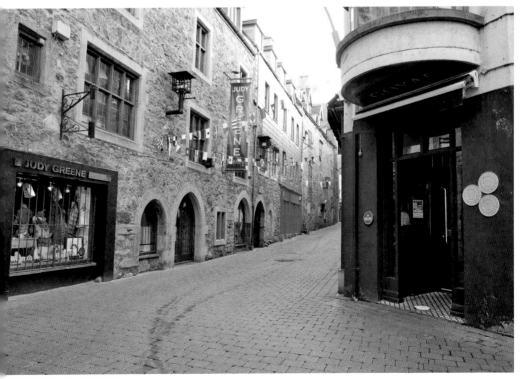

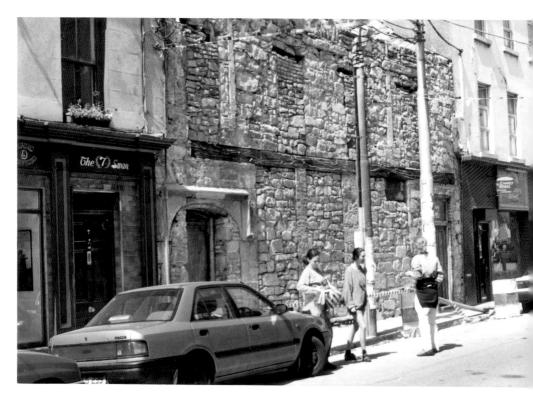

Upper Cross Street, *c.* 1990

The site today occupied by Busker Browne's bar on Upper Cross Street has long been associated with the Dominican nuns who, in 1686, aquired the property from John Kirwan. In fact, a portion of the present bar is called 'the slate nunnery'. The site, which contained the remains of four late medieval houses, was renovated in the early 1990s. Busker Brownes opened in 1994.

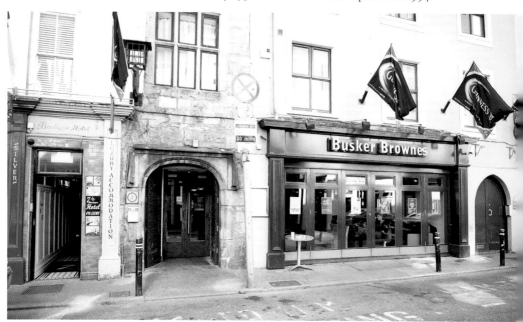

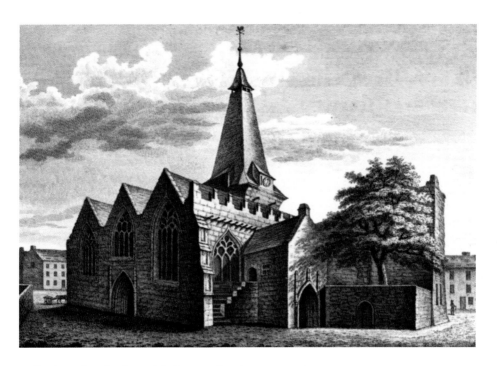

Collegiate Church of St Nicholas, Lombard Street, *c.* 1820

Dedicated to St Nicholas of Myra, a saint associated with seaport churches, this building can trace its origins to 1320. Columbus is said to have prayed here in 1477 before setting out for the New World; this is substantiated by the fact that a Galway man named Rice de Culvy accompanied the Italian explorer on his epic voyage. In 1652, following the siege of Galway, Cromwellian forces used the church as a stable for their horses. The church has been much developed and embellished over the centuries. On 23 November 1883 its wooden steeple was struck by lightening. The clock was added to the replacement steeple in 1898.

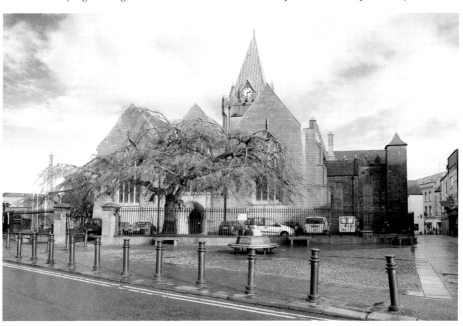

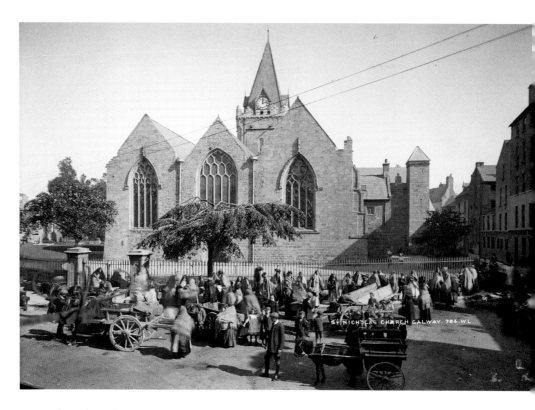

Egg and Fowl Market, Lombard Street, c. 1890
In the late nineteenth century a busy egg and fowl market operated around the Collegiate church of St Nicholas, on Church Street, Lombard Street and Market Street. Here Galwegians purchased not only eggs and fowl, but other farm and sea produce such as butter and dillisk. A pictorial map of Galway, dating from 1651, shows a market cross located in front of the collegiate church indicating that the market is of ancient origin.

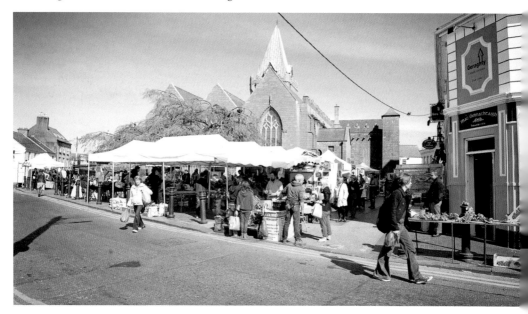

Lynch's Memorial, Market Street, c. 1905

One of Galway's most famous landmarks, the Lynch Memorial is in fact a mere 'tourist trap' based on an unsubstantiated folk tale in which a Galway Mayor hangs his own son for the murder of a Spanish visitor. Erected in 1854, its inscription reads: 'This ancient memorial of the stern and unbending justice of the chief magistrate of this city, James Lynch Fitzstephen, elected mayor A.D. 1493, who condemned and executed his own guilty son Walter on this spot, has been restored to this its ancient site A.D. 1854 with the approval of the Town Commissioners by the chairman, V. Revd. Peter Daly, P.P. and Vicar of St. Nicholas.'

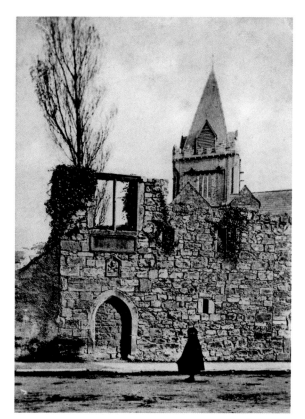

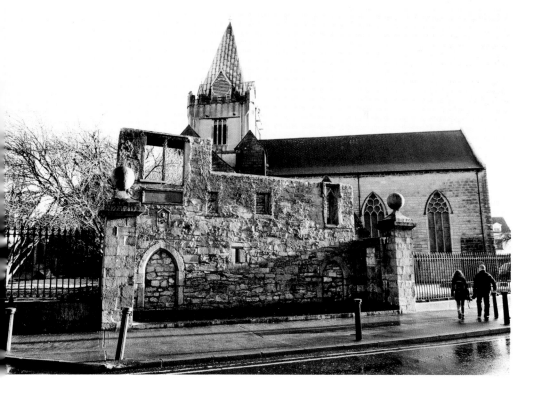

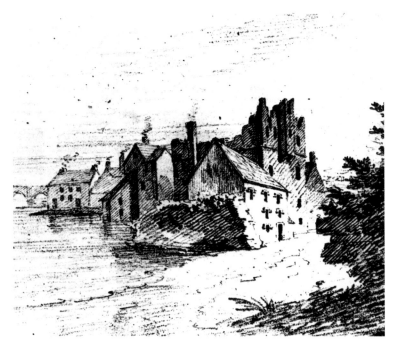

Blake's Castle, Quay Street, 1700s & c. 1975
At the southern end of Quay Street, near the Fish Market, stands Blake's Castle, a sixteenth-century, urban tower house. It served as the Galway County Gaol from 1686 to 1810, by which time the new town and county gaols were built at Nun's Island on the site of what is now Galway Cathedral. The castle became part of Burke's Distillery for a period and more recently housed an ESB substation. In the 1990s the castle was reconstructed and converted into a restaurant.

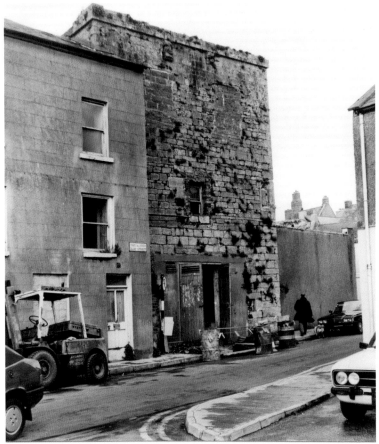

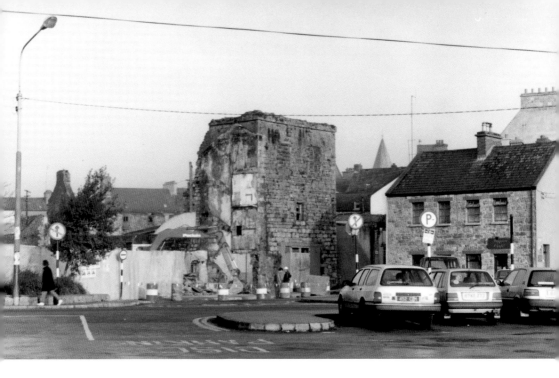

Blake's Castle, Quay Street, c. 1992
In the early 1990s McDonogh's Chemical Works, which stood on the site formerly occupied by Burke's Distillery, was razed to the ground to make way for a Jury's Inn hotel. The chemical works had manufactured superphosphates and sulphuric acid onsite for fertiliser. The hotel opened in April 1993 and, along with the Portmore development and reconstruction of Blake's Castle, it transformed this area of the town beyond recognition.

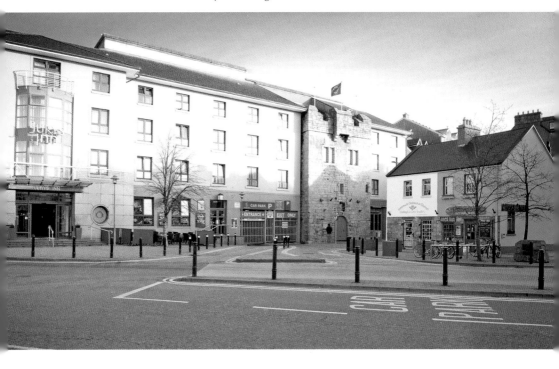

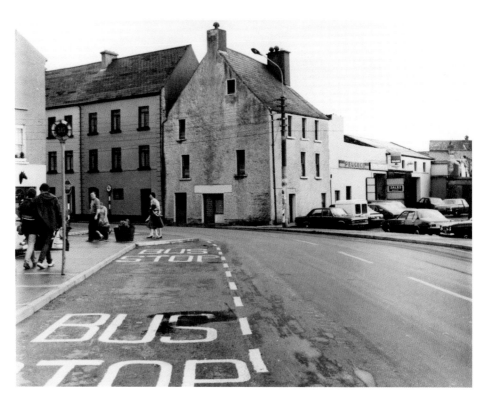

Flood Street & Spanish Parade, *c.* 1975
From the late eighteenth century onwards, a small open square near to the old quays became known as the 'Spanish Parade'. In 1820, Galway historian James Hardiman wrote that the square derived this name from the fact it was the place 'where Spanish merchants were formerly accustomed to assemble'. Since this photograph was taken, a new road called Spanish Parade was constructed through the square.

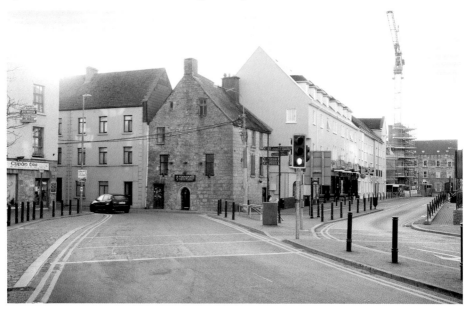

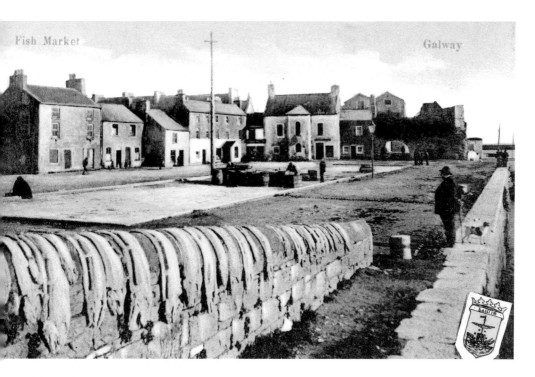

Fish Market, *c.* 1905

Before 1800, the town's fish market was held at the east end of the West Bridge, now O'Brien's Bridge. General Meyrick, the military governor of Galway, persuaded the wealthier inhabitants of the town to contribute towards the provision of a more suitably located fish market. The open area in front of the Spanish Arch, the site of the medieval quays, was chosen. Over its entrance was an inscription: 'This fish market was built by subscription, under the patronage of General Meyrick, who during his residence here, acquired the praise of a people, for his administration of justice and benevolence.'

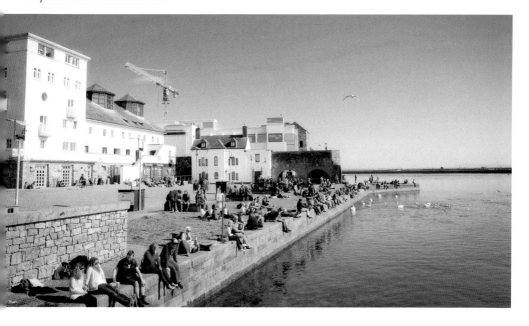

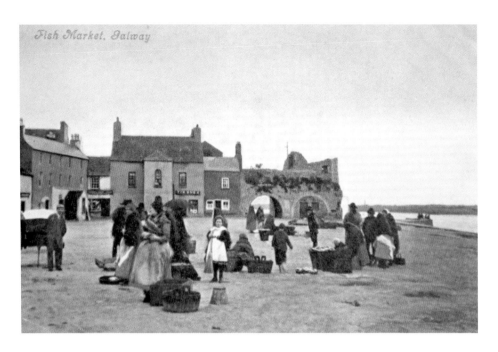

Fish Market, *c.* 1900

The Fish Market was dominated by women from the Claddagh who sold the fish caught by their husbands, sons and brothers. The fish were gutted and the offal discarded at the market. One of the side effects of this unhealthy practice was the contamination of the local water supply, the River Corrib. Visitors to the town were often afflicted by a disorder, known as the Galway, if those fetching water did so from the vicinity of the Fish Market rather than at Nun's Island, upriver of the town.

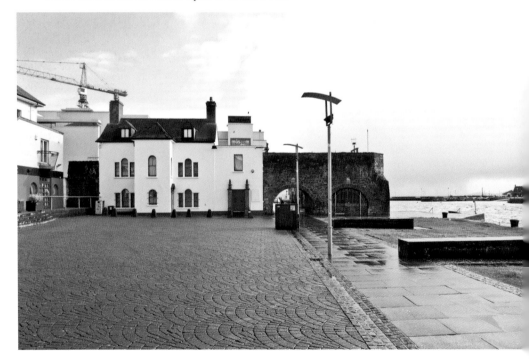

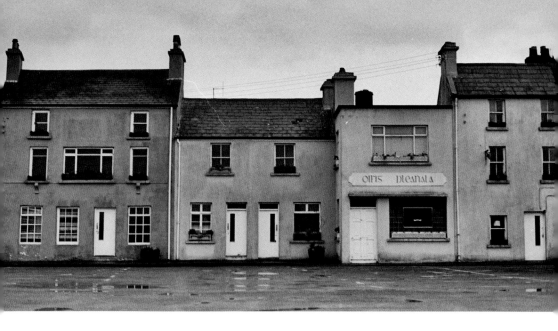

Fish Market, 1981
Significant developments that have taken place in recent decades in and around the area known as the Fish Market. In the late 1980s, archaeologists digging in the vicinity uncovered remnants of the medieval docks and old town walls. Despite some objections, the controversial and gargantuan Portmore development (locally referred to as 'Madonna's Bra') was built over the structures.

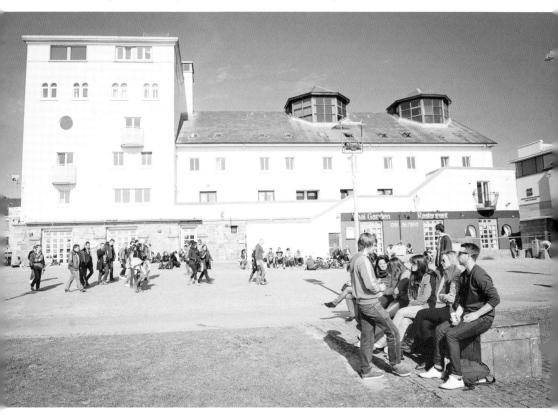

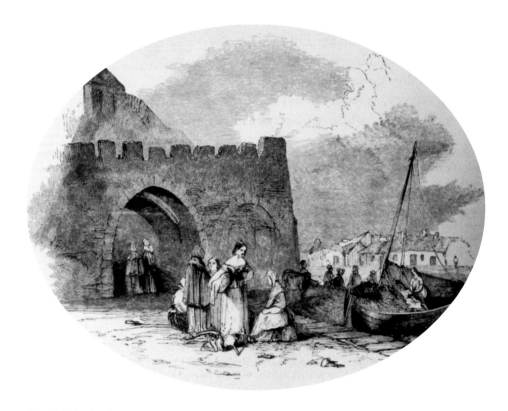

Spanish Arch, 1843

These medieval structures are known as the Spanish Arch and the Blind Arch (as it is closed up). The adjoining building was, at the dawn of the twentieth century, Tim Shea's public house. Sculptress and writer Clare Consuelo Sheridan (1885–1970) lived and worked here between 1948 and 1954. In 1971 Galway Corporation bought the property to serve as a city museum which opened in 1976.

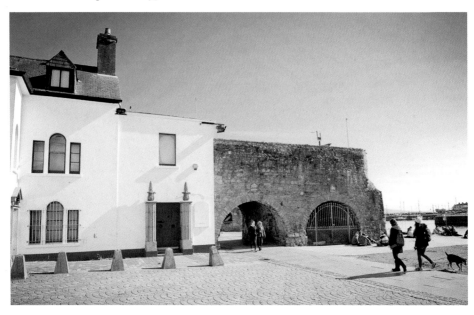

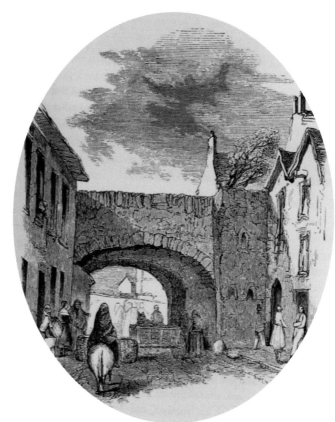

Spanish Arch (Rear), 1854
The so-called Spanish Arch evolved from an extension to the medieval walls built to protect the medieval quays called *Ceann-an-Bhalla*, or Wallshead. In 1584, a bulwark was built here, under the direction of Nicholas Malby, Lord President of Connaught, in order to strengthen Galway's defences, as tensions were escalating between Protestant Queen Elizabeth I of England and Catholic King Philip II of Spain. There were once four arches, but they were partially destroyed in 1755 by a tsunami generated by an earthquake off the coast of Lisbon in Portugal.

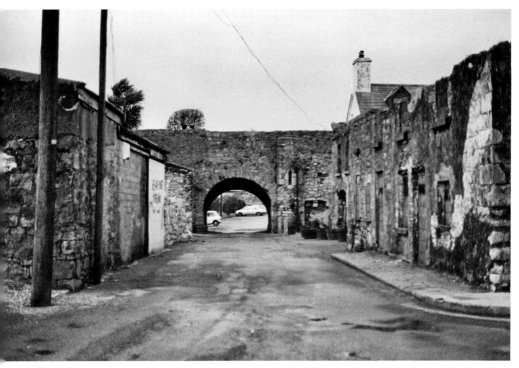

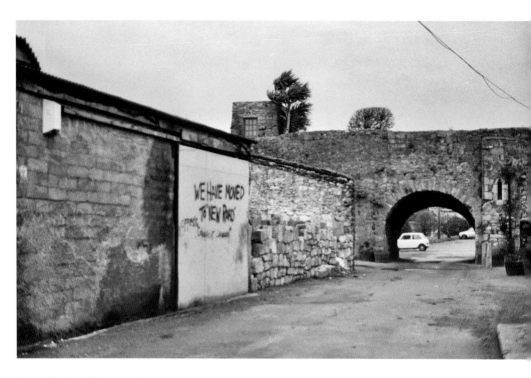

Spanish Arch (Rear), 1981
As with the Fish Market to the north of the Spanish Arch, the area to the rear of the arch has also been transformed in recent decades. A garage was replaced by Nimmo's restaurant and wine bar in 1992, which was in turn replaced by Ard Bia at Nimmo's restaurant in 2008.

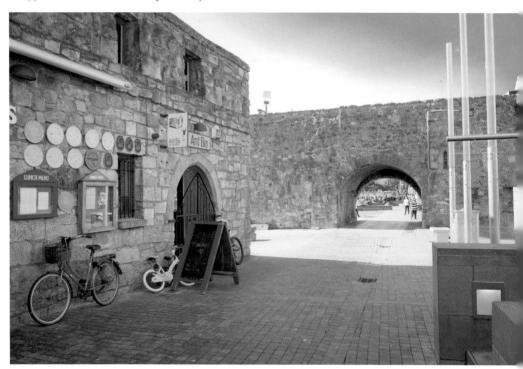

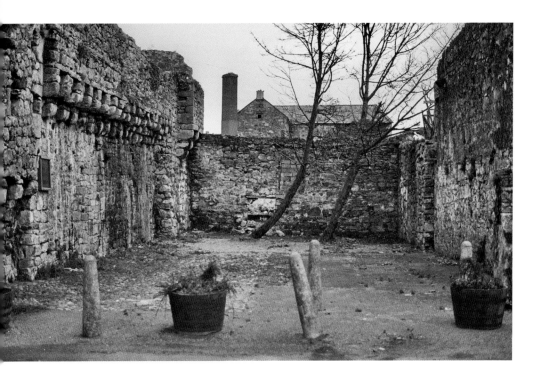

Ceann an Bhalla, 1981

In the late thirteenth century, the Anglo-Norman de Burghs, who had established a settlement on the banks of the River Corrib, collected taxes for the building of town walls, which eventually enclosed an area of around 13 hectares, or 32 acres. Over the centuries the walls were maintained or rebuilt as needed. Most of the fortifications have been demolished since the late eighteenth century, by which time large-scale wall building had come to an end.

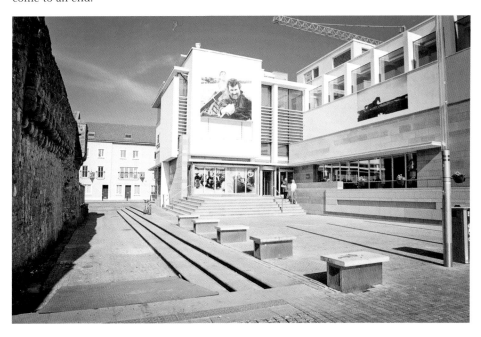

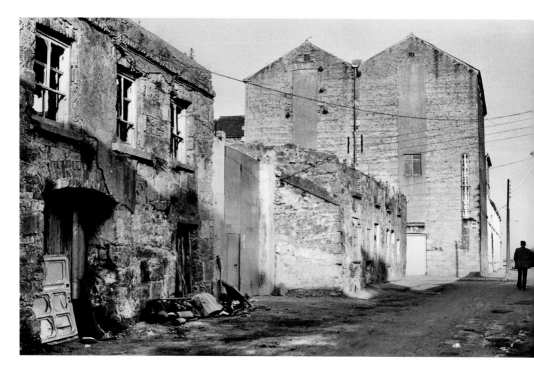

Long Walk, 1981

In the early twentieth century the boatbuilding yard of John Francis Reney, who was regarded as the last of the traditional Claddagh boatbuilders, was located by the Spanish Arch. It was here that, in 1922, Reney built the famous *Truelight* boat – the last of the Claddagh Hookers. In the early 2000s, Galway City Museum was built between the Spanish Arch and the Long Walk. As a Galway City Council initiative, it was officially opened in April 2007.

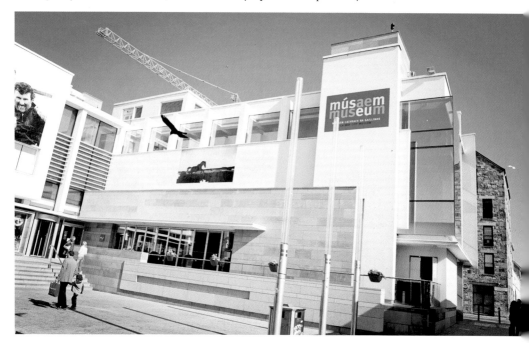

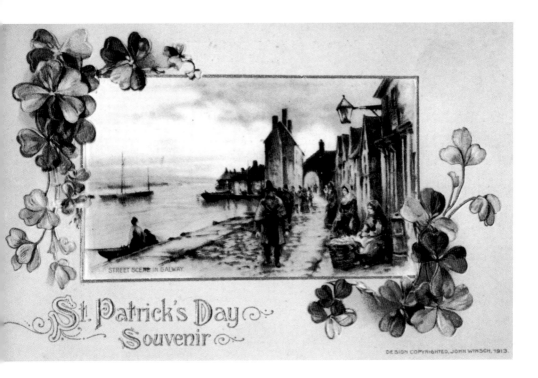

STREET SCENE IN GALWAY

St. Patrick's Day Souvenir

DESIGN COPYRIGHTED, JOHN WINSCH, 1913.

Long Walk, 1913

In 1651 the Long Walk was a mere jetty of stones leading from the Blind Arch to a place known as *Carraig an Phréacháin*, the Crow's Rock. In 1670 Edward Eyre, a Cromwellian adventurist, acquired extensive properties outside the walls of the town, including roughly the areas around Woodquay, Eyre Square, Victoria Place, Forthill and Merchants Road. Included in the lease was this wall walk, which became known during its development as the Long Wall and then Eyre's Long Walk. The dock at the end of the Long Walk, today known as the Mud Dock, was formerly called Eyre's Dock.

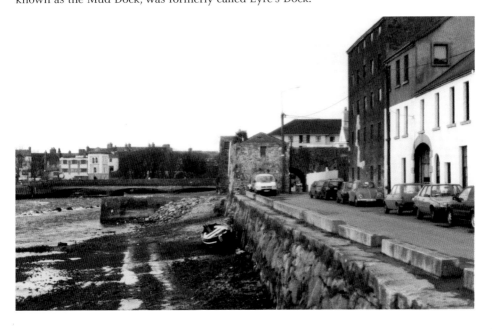

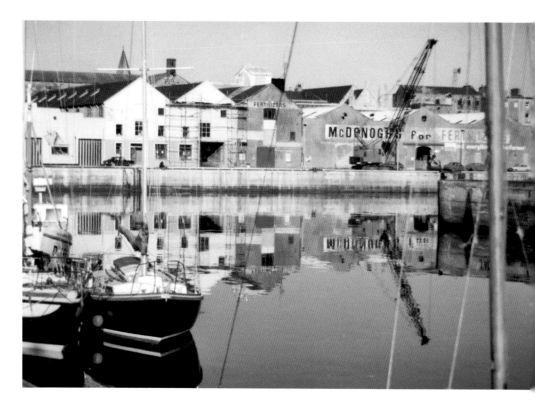

Galway Docks, 1980s

In the early nineteenth century ships docked at the medieval quays or at the Mud Dock (the Old Dock) at the end of Long Walk. In 1837, Galway's main exports were corn, flour, kelp, marble and wool, and the principal imports were timber, wine, salt, coal, hemp, tallow and iron. Originally known as the New Docks, the Commercial Dock was finished in 1842 at a cost of more than £40,000. Completed in 2002, the Dockgate development replaced McDonogh Fertilizers, which had shadowed the docks for much of the twentieth century.

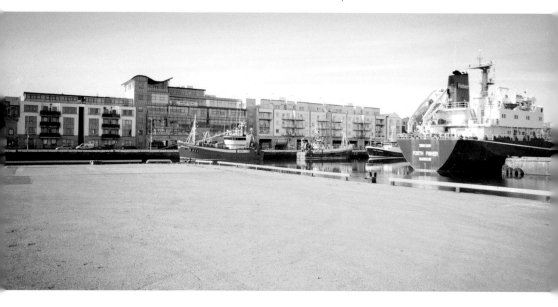

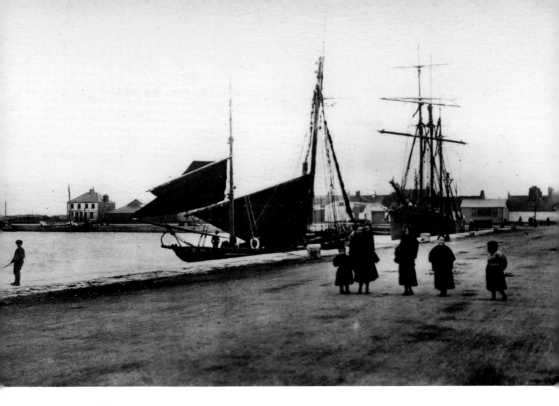

New Dock Road, c. 1900

In the 1850s there was much excitement at the prospect of Galway – some 400 kilometres closer to New York than Liverpool – becoming a mail packet station and the main seaport for all transatlantic traffic between Europe and North America. However, the venture was short-lived and beset by ill-luck and tragedy. In the 1880s, a deep-water dock named the Dún Aengus Dock was constructed that was merged with the Commercial Dock in the 1960s. More recently, in 2009 and 2012, Galway Docks was a port of call for the Volvo Ocean Race. Today, the Dún Aengus apartment complex dominates the dock's western skyline.

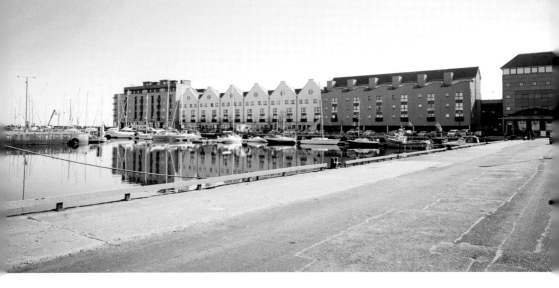

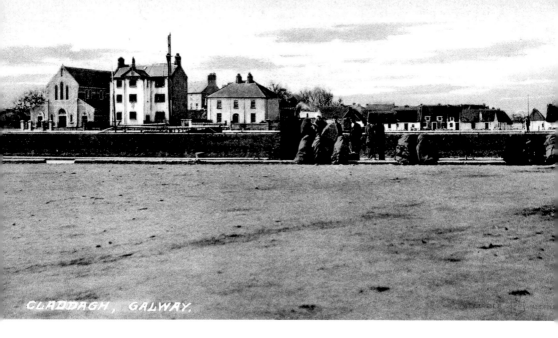

CLADDAGH, GALWAY.

Claddagh & *Garraí Glas*, *c.* 1900
Galway historian James Hardiman wrote that the Claddagh, situated outside the medieval town walls, 'is supposed, with every probability, to have been occupied as a fishing station, since the first peopling of this island'. The village derived its name from the Irish word *Cladach*, meaning a foreshore. *Garraí Glas*, meaning 'green garden' in Irish, was situated on the edge of Claddagh.

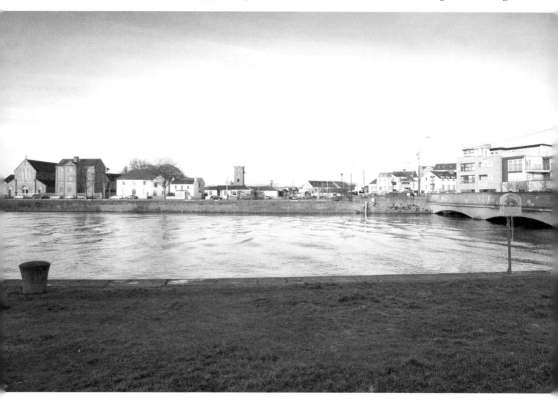

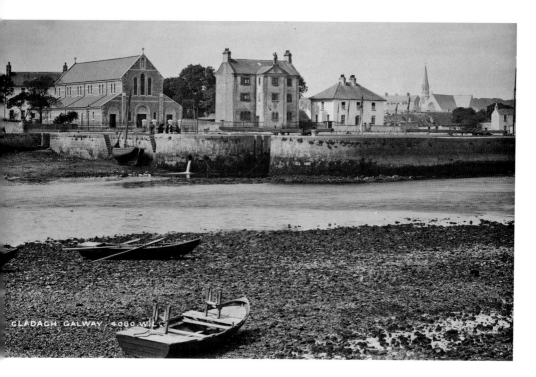

Church of St Mary's and Piscatorial School, Claddagh, *c.* 1900

Dedicated on 25 October 1891, the Roman Catholic church of St Mary on the Hill was designed by the ecclesiastical architect William Hague. To the right is the Piscatorial School, founded by the Dominican Fathers in 1846 specifically to teach the children of the Claddagh village new fishing techniques in the hope of developing the industry. By 1887 it was operating as an ordinary national school. In recent decades, the building served as a labour exchange.

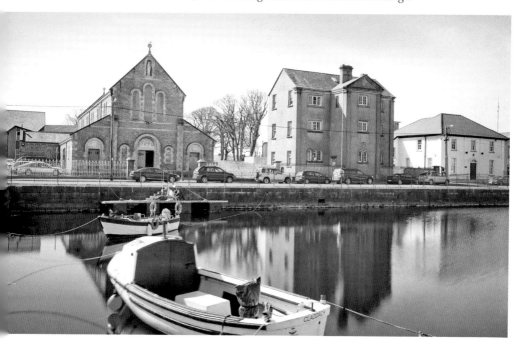

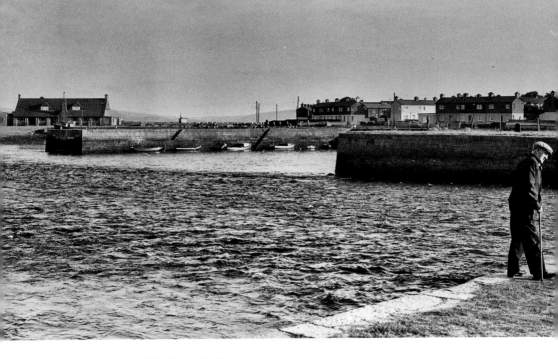

Corrib Estuary and Claddagh Hall, 1981

On 2 December 1912, Claddagh Hall was officially opened by Dr Thomas O'Dea, Bishop of Galway. An initiative of the local Dominican Fathers, the community hall was part-funded by the Congested District Board. It was to be a venue for local fishermen to meet and discuss their mutual interests. As with the Piscatorial School, it was hoped that the initiative would encourage those who relied on the sea to modernise their fishing techniques. Within two years of its opening, during the First World War, most of the young men of the village were serving overseas with the Royal Navy.

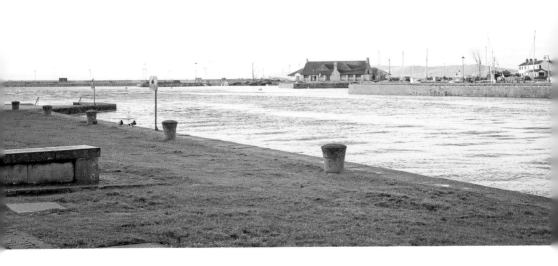

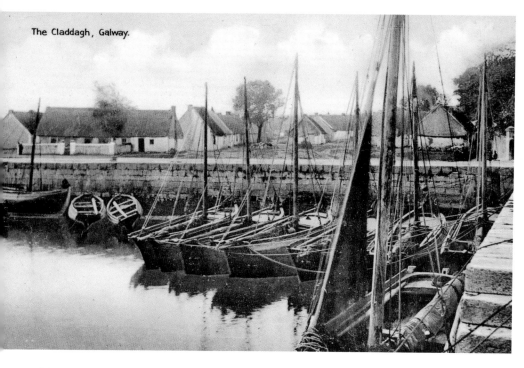

The Claddagh, Galway.

Ballyknow Quay, Claddagh, *c.* 1905
The upper pier, known as Ballyknow Quay, forms one side of the Claddagh Basin. The lower pier was known as Claddagh Quay. Both Claddagh and Ballyknow quays were repaired between 1843 and 1851 and were linked to Nimmo's Pier by 1852.

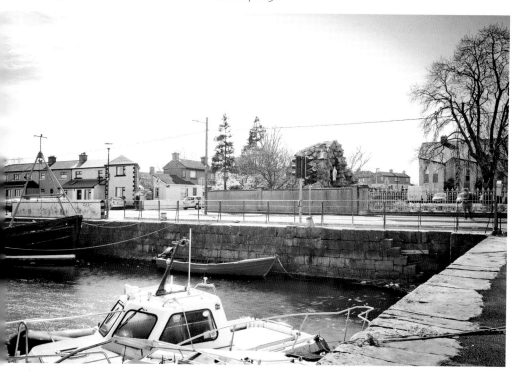

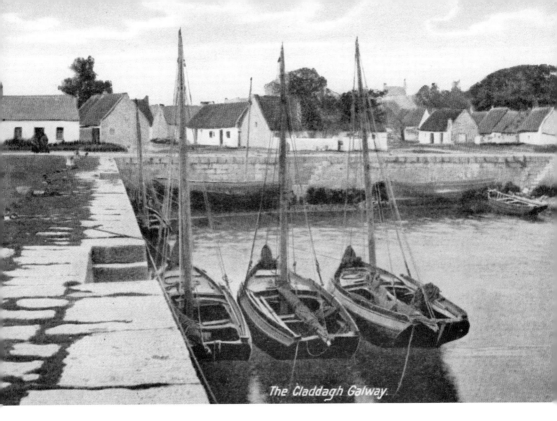

Claddagh Quay, Claddagh, *c*. 1905
The Claddagh fishing fleet docked at Ballyknow Quay and Claddagh Quay. In 1836 there were 820 Claddagh fishermen operating 105 sailing craft – hookers of various sizes – and a further 80 rowing boats. The fishermen dealt in herring, mackerel, skad, turbot, haddock, sole, hake, cod, ling, bream, gurnet and pilchards.

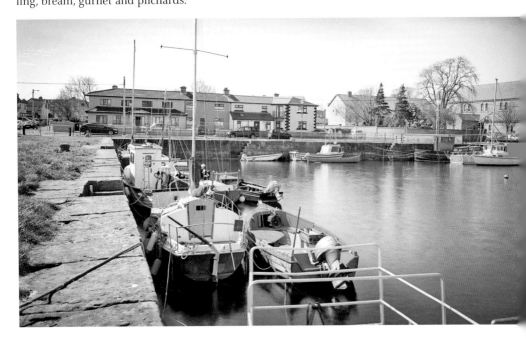

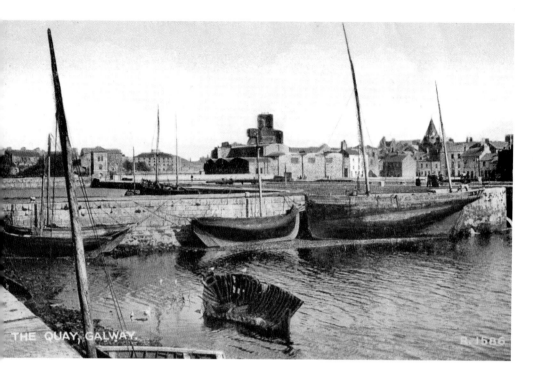

THE QUAY, GALWAY.

R.1586

Claddagh Basin, Claddagh, 1940s

Officially opened by Lord Eglinton, Lord Lieutenant of Ireland in August 1852, the Eglinton Canal connected Galway Bay to the Upper Corrib via the Claddagh Basin. The 1-kilometre canal was constructed as the river current was too fast and strong, and its bed too shallow for navigation through the town. Canal locks were constructed in the Claddagh Basin and Parkavera, at which boats ascended from the level of the sea to that of Lough Corrib. In 1954 the canal's swing bridges were replaced by fixed ones so that it is no longer navigable.

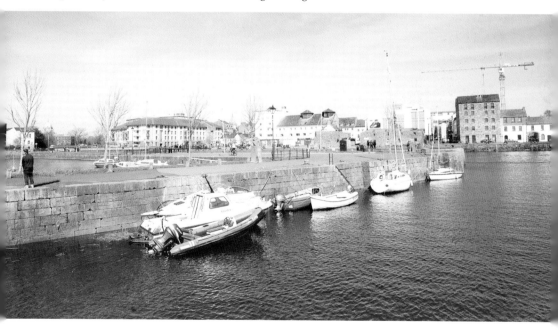

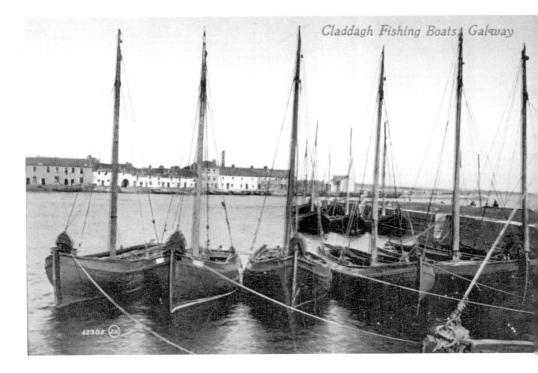

Claddagh Fishing Boats Galway

Claddagh Fishing Boats & Long Walk, *c.* 1909

The fishermen of the Claddagh had many superstitions and taboos associated with the sea and fishing. They had a particular aversion to foxes, hares and rabbits (all of which are *rua*, or red-haired). The sight of a fox was enough to prevent them fishing on the best of days, even when all ready to sail. They would never utter the names of those animals and did not like to hear their names spoken by others. An old Claddagh curse went as follows: A fox on your fish hook and a hare on your bait!

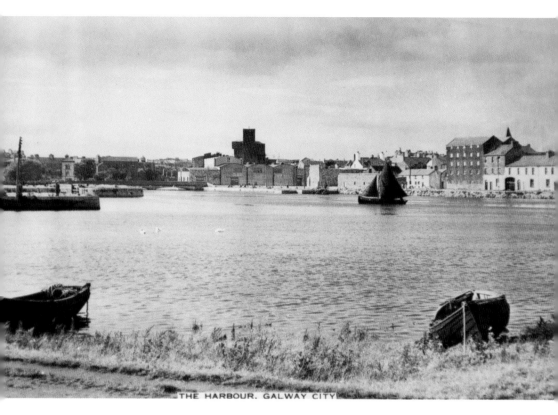

Galway from Nimmo's Pier, 1950s
The arched warehouses and towering silo of McDonogh's Chemical Works dominates the background, between the Fisheries Tower (*left*) and the spire of the church of St Nicholas (*right*). Today, Jury's Inn hotel occupies this space.

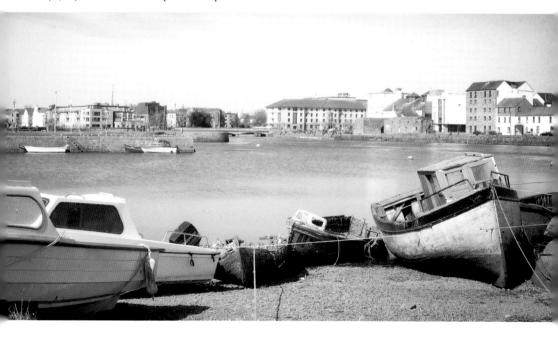

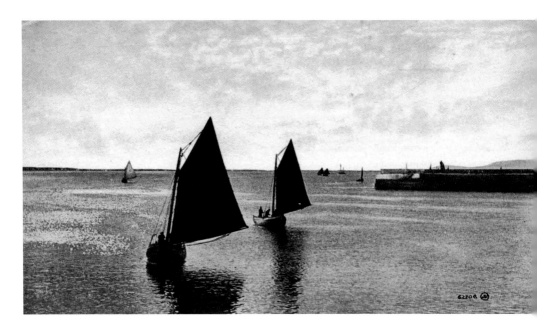

Claddagh Hookers Rounding Nimmo's Pier, *c.* **1909**
Alexander Nimmo (1783–1832) designed and erected many small piers around the Galway coastline, while engineer to the Irish Board of Fisheries. Nimmo's Pier was built in the 1820s and extends from Claddagh Quay southwards past Ringhanane Quay. As well as being an asset to the Claddagh, it afforded protection to the old quays at the Spanish Arch, sheltering it from southerly gales that often wrecked boats moored there.

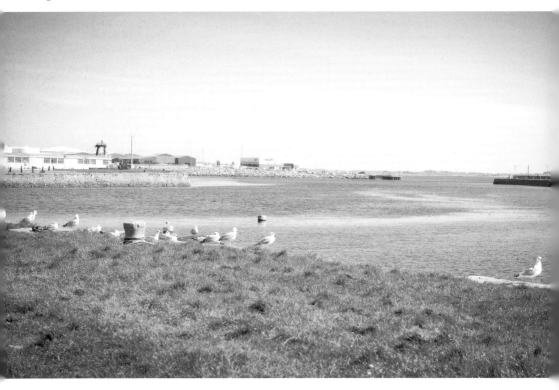

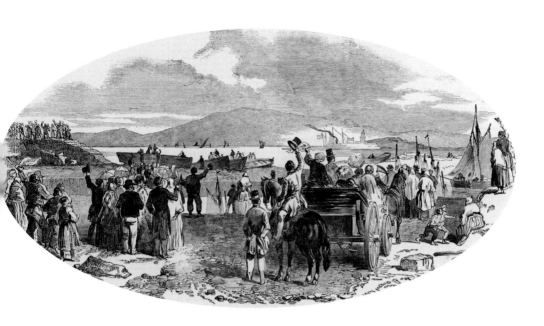

Mutton Island & Galway Bay, 1850

Originally known as *Inis Caorach*, meaning Sheep Island, this small 2-acre island, situated at the entrance to Galway harbour, has long been used to control access to the town by sea. In 1652, a fort on the island was to be given up under the terms of surrender to Cromwell's forces. A castellated tower on the island was demolished in 1815 to make way for a new lighthouse. In the early 2000s, a waste treatment plant was opened on the island and a causeway was constructed linking the island to the mainland at South Park, known locally as the 'Swamp'.

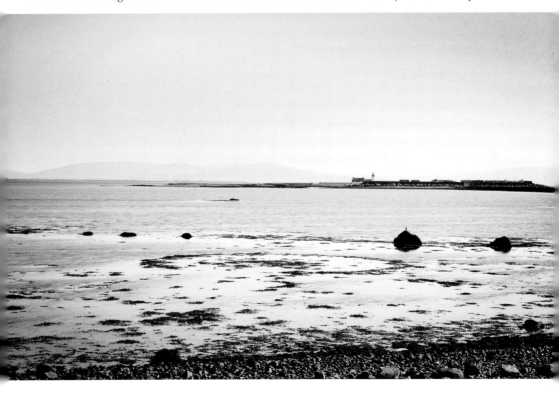

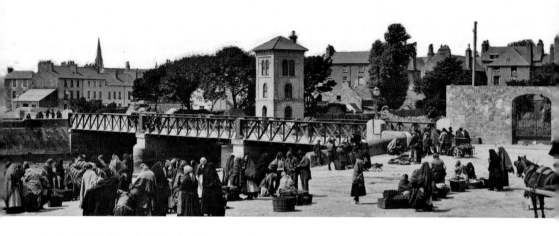

Claddagh Bridge & Fisheries Tower, c. 1890
Completed in 1853, the Fisheries Tower was originally a draft netting station. It was built by brothers Edmund and Thomas Ashworth from Lancashire, who came from a prominent Quaker family of cotton manufacturers. In 1852 they purchased the Galway Fishery, extending from Lough Corrib to the sea, for £5,000, and established the world's first commercial salmon fishery. Galway Civic Trust restored the tower in the late 1990s for use as an exhibition space.

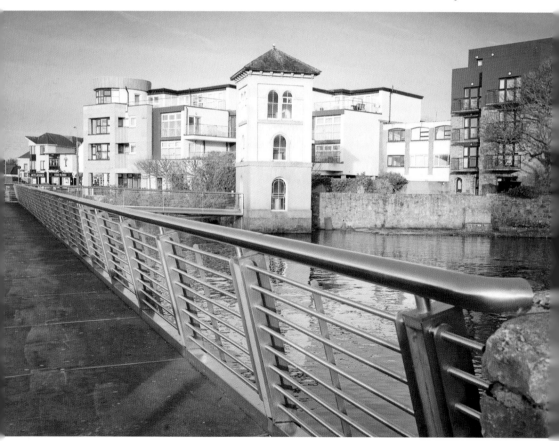

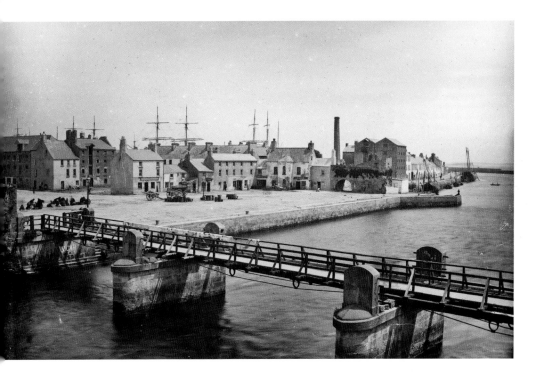

Claddagh Bridge and Fishmarket, *c.* 1880

Prior to the construction of the Eglinton Canal, completed in 1852, there was no bridge directly linking the Claddagh with the town. To cross the River Corrib, Claddagh residents had to go via Dominick Street and the West Bridge (now O'Brien's Bridge). During the construction of the Eglinton Canal, the Board of Works built a temporary wooden bridge to transport building materials from the town at Fish Market to the Claddagh. Originally known as the Claddagh Bridge, it was replaced by an iron bridge in 1887 and by the concrete Wolfe Tone Bridge in 1934.

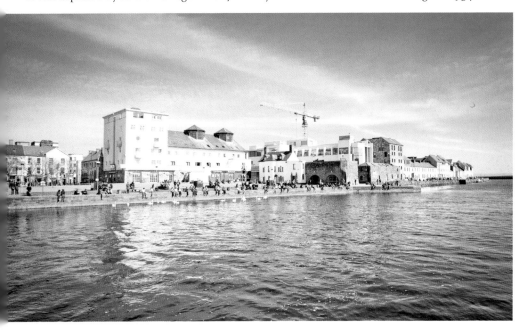

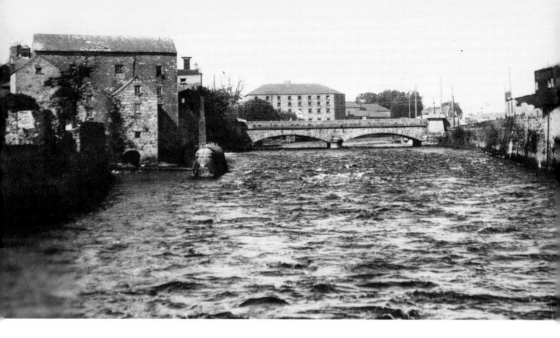

William O'Brien Bridge

In 1442 Edmond Lynch Fitz-Thomas built a bridge at his own expense over the Corrib, which was called the West or Great Bridge. He was known as *Emon-an-Tuane* (Edmond of the Tuns) because of the vast quantity of foreign wines he imported. The bridge is today replaced by O'Brien's Bridge named for William O'Brien (1852–1928), politician and land agitator, who served time in Galway County Gaol. A plaque set into the western pier reads: 'William O'Brien Bridge by resolution passed by the Town Commissioners during his imprisonment in Galway jail A.D. 1889.'

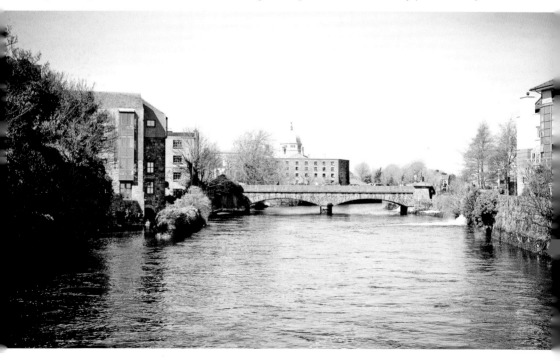

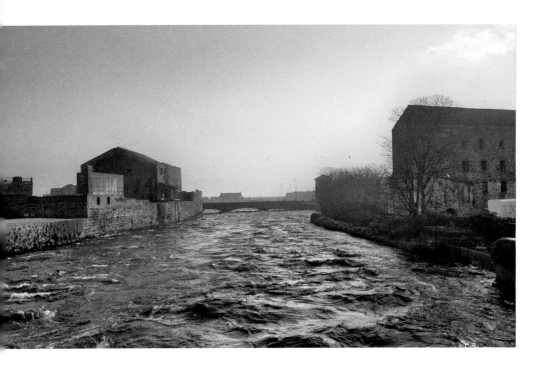

Wolfe Tone Bridge, 1981
The River Corrib is seen here flanked by derelict buildings. To the left – the east bank – is McDonogh's Chemical Works, built on the former site of Burke's Distillery. Founded by Edward Cussen Burke, this distillery was in operation from the 1820s until the middle of the century, after which time it lay in ruins. In the early 1990s the extensive site was redeveloped as a Jury's Inn hotel and an apartment complex.

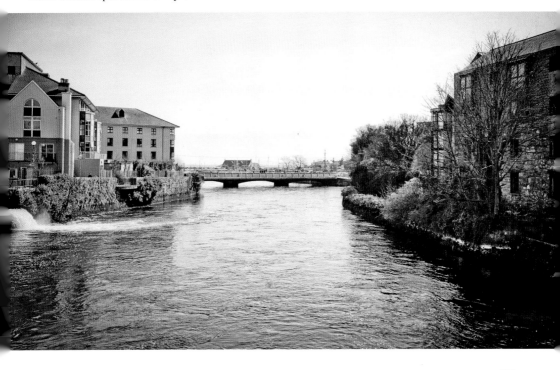

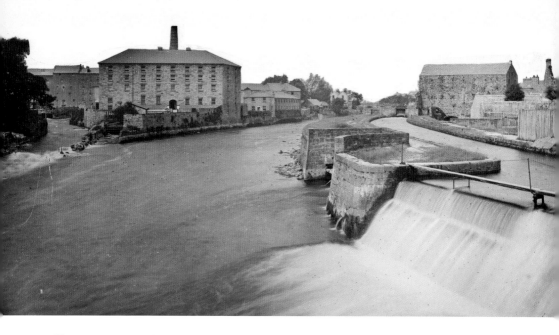

Mill Course & Persse's Nun's Island Distillery, *c.* 1900
The original Nuns Island Distillery (*left*) was opened in 1815 by Patrick Joyce and was, at that time, the only one in Connacht. In 1840, Burton Persse bought the distillery from the Encumbered Estates Court and converted it into a woollen mill. Persse already owned two distilleries; however, when his lease on his Newcastle Distillery lapsed and the woollen trade declined, he restored the works at Nun's Island to its original business. In the late 1880s the distillery had an annual output of 400,000 gallons of Persse's Galway Whiskey.

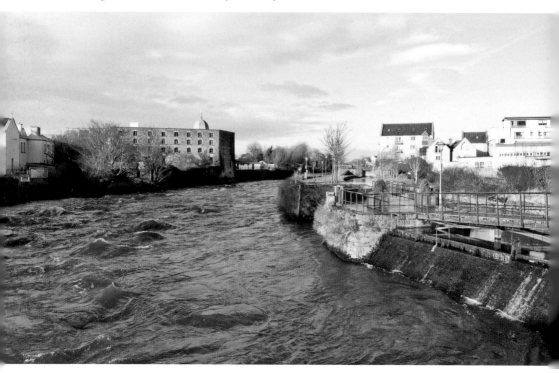

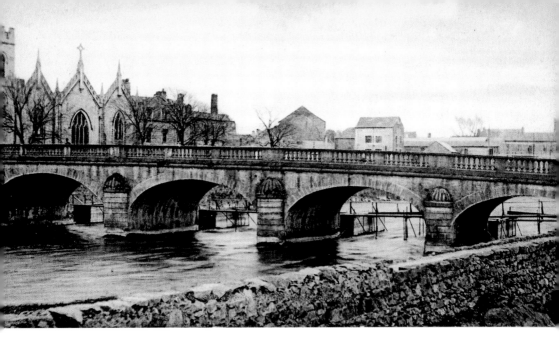

Salmon Weir Bridge, 1900s

Constructed between 1818 and 1819 to connect the new county courthouse at Newtownsmith to the new gaols on Nun's Island, Salmon Weir Bridge was originally known as New Bridge or Gaol Bridge. During salmon season, the bridge afforded the best vantage point from which to view the annual phenomenon of salmon migrating upriver. The chapel of St Vincent's Convent of Mercy, at the east end of the bridge, was for many years known as 'Daly's Chapel' after Father Peter Daly (c. 1788–1868) who had invited the Sisters of Mercy to establish a convent at Galway.

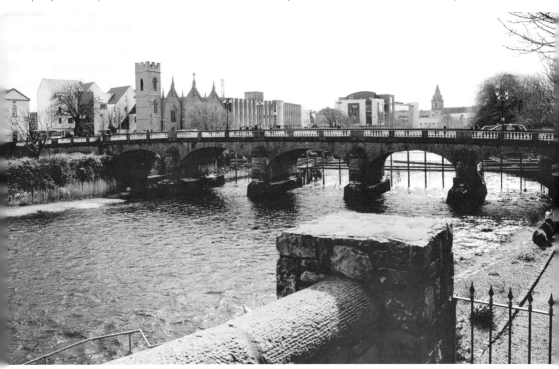

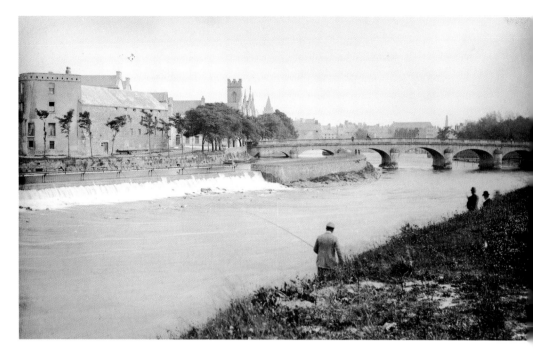

Salmon Fisheries, *c.* 1900

Galway Fishery is a freshwater and tidal fishery extending from Lough Corrib to the sea. It was, according to Galway historian James Hardiman, 'one of most valuable in the kingdom'. The fishery, first mentioned in 1283 during the reign of Edward I, changed hands many times over the centuries. In 1852 it was purchased by the Ashworth brothers from Lancashire through the Encumbered Estates Court for £5,000.

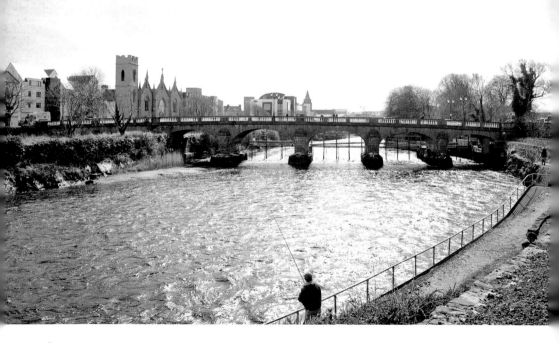

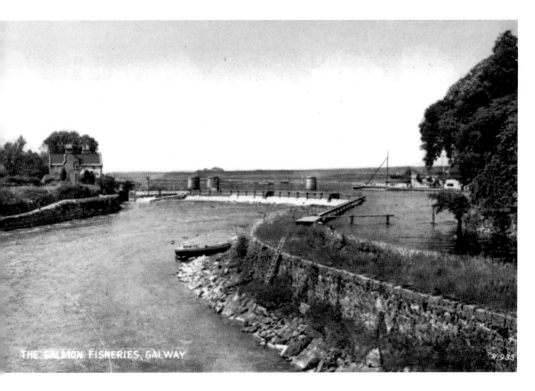

Weir Lodge & Salmon Fisheries, 1940s

Weir Lodge is a late nineteenth century Gothic-style house overlooking the salmon fisheries, which today houses the Western Fisheries Board. Weir House is located a little downriver of the lodge. Built in 1823, it houses the Galway County Club, which was formerly located at Eyre Square.

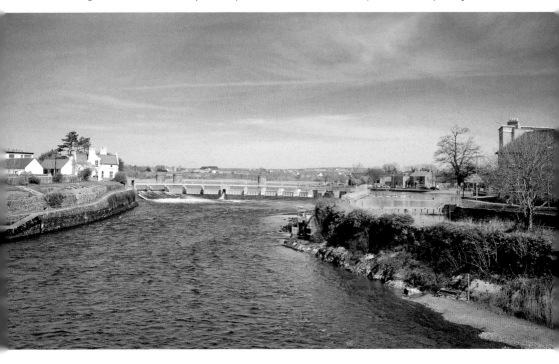

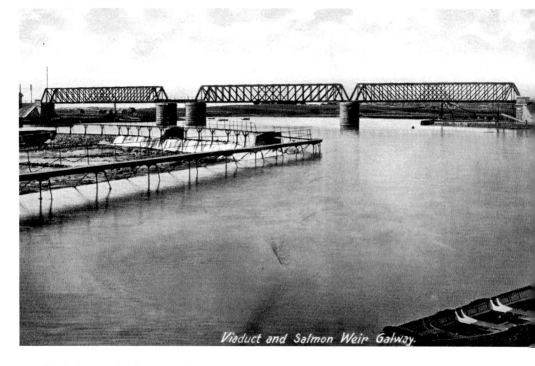

Corrib Viaduct and Salmon Weir, 1900s
The Galway to Clifden Railway was inaugurated in 1895. It was constructed as a relief work by the Midland Great Western Railway Company under Arthur J. Balfour, the British Chief Secretary for Ireland. The Corrib Viaduct, which carried the railway over the River Corrib, consisted of three spans, each of 45 metres between bearings. The line closed in April 1935 and the ironwork was sold as scrap.

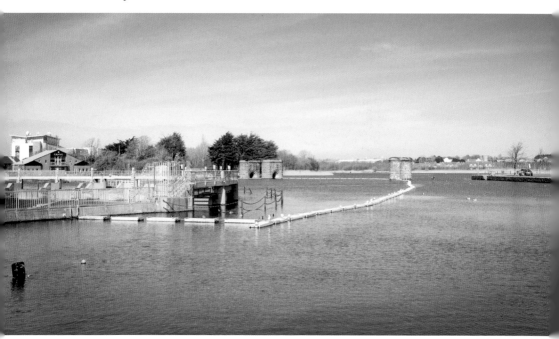

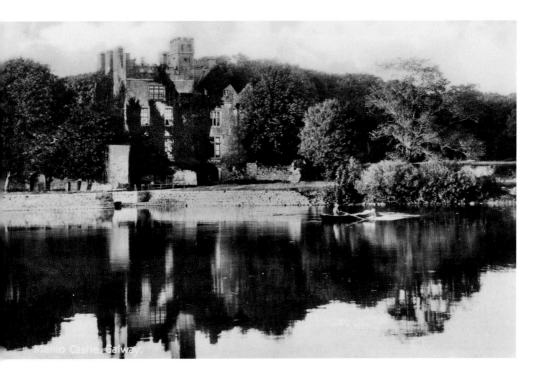

Menlo Castle, *c.* 1910
Menlo, or Menlough, derives from the Irish Mionlach meaning 'small lake'. The ruins of Menlo Castle are situated on the banks of the River Corrib approximately 3 kilometres upstream of the city. The original tower house was built in the mid-sixteenth century and became the seat of the Blake family, one of the Tribes of Galway. Tragically, in 1910, the house was destroyed in an accidental fire.

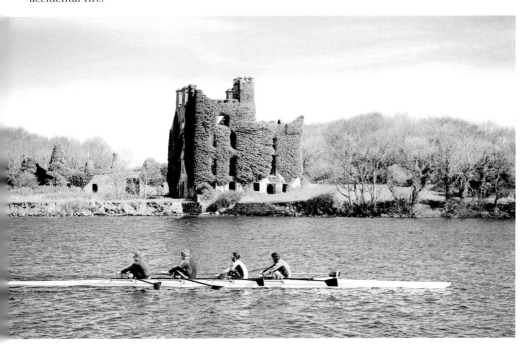

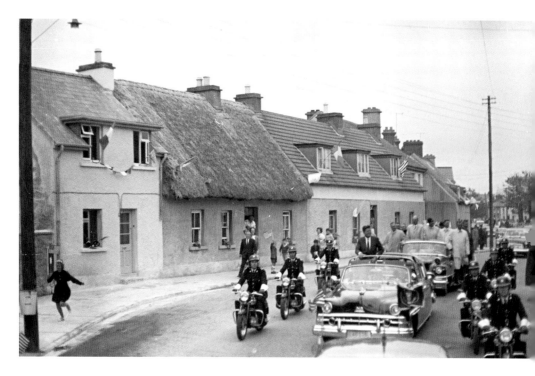

Presidential Motorcade, Lower Salthill, 1963

On 29 June 1963 US President John F. Kennedy visited Galway as part of a four-day trip to Ireland. He was made a Freeman of Galway at a ceremony in Eyre Square before departing for Salthill. He concluded his emotive speech saying: 'I must say that though other days may not be so bright, as we look toward the future, that the brightest days will continue to be those we spent with you here in Ireland.' He was assassinated less than five months later. In 1965, the park within Eyre Square was renamed John F. Kennedy Memorial Park.

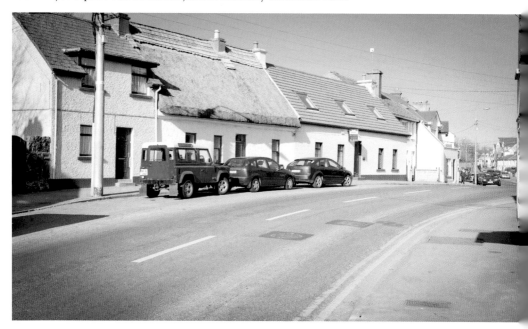

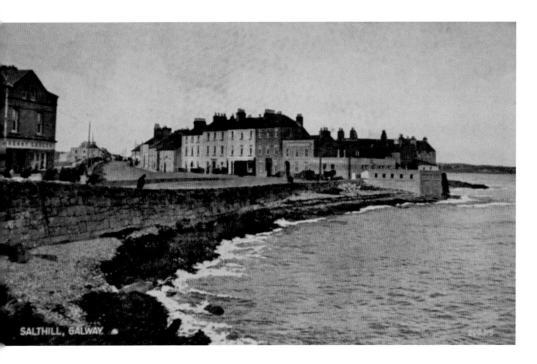

Salthill, 1920s & 1970s

Known in Irish as *Bóthar na Trá*, or Strand Road, the suburban seaside resort of Salthill has been attracting visitors seeking 'the health restoring benefits of sea-bathing' since the early nineteenth century. In 1815, the resort was described as a 'delightful spot, so invigorating and health restoring and so calculated to rouse the spirits of the invalid and impart renewed energies to those who have been engaged throughout the years attending to laborious duties and the fatigues of life.'

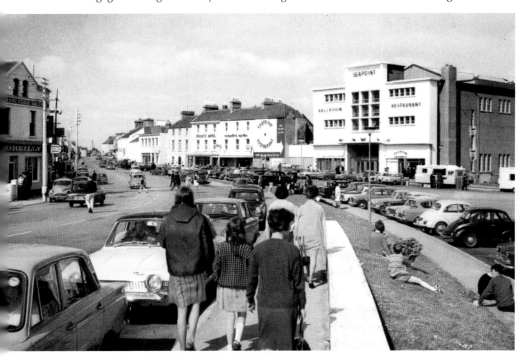

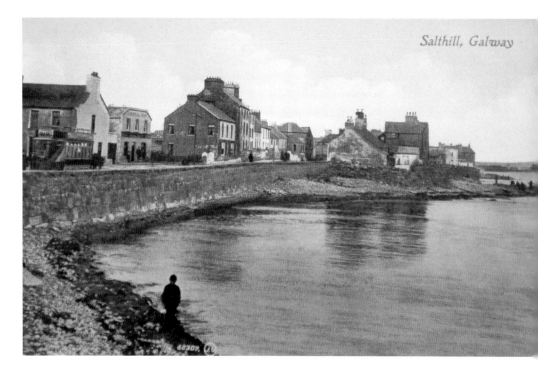

Salthill, Galway

Salthill, 1900s

In 1925, two men visiting Galway were arrested by Gardaí at Blackrock in Salthill for bathing without costumes. The case was brought before the Galway Urban Council who debated whether or not to take proceedings against the pair. It was eventually decided that warning signs were not sufficiently well displayed and it was decided not to prosecute the men as they were visitors who were probably not aware of the regulations. In 1971 a local senator battled to have bikini-clad girls excluded from Blackrock as he thought they were a source of embarrassment for priests and older men.

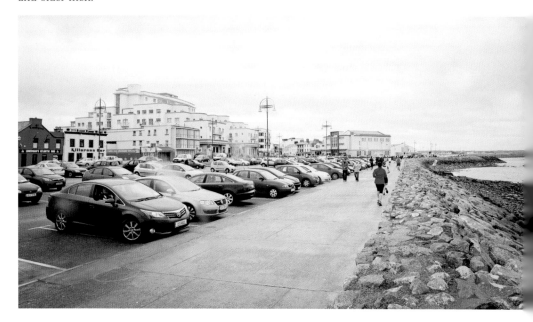

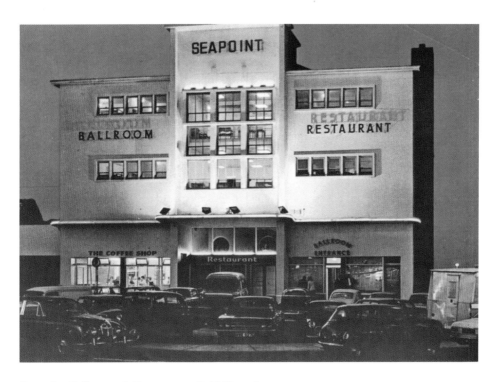

Seapoint Ballroom & Restaurant, Salthill, 1960s

When Seapoint opened in 1949 it was the largest venue of its kind in the west of Ireland. The dance floor was capable of accommodating 2,000 dancers and the restaurant could seat 350 diners. In the 1950s and '60s the venue played host to the biggest dance bands and showbands. By the early 1980s Seapoint was struggling to compete with fully-licensed discos and it formally closed in 1985. Herb Miller (brother of Glenn) and his nineteen-piece orchestra played the final bash.

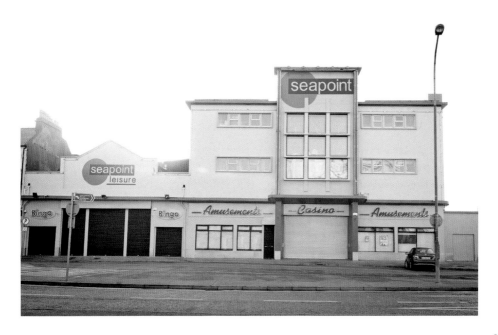

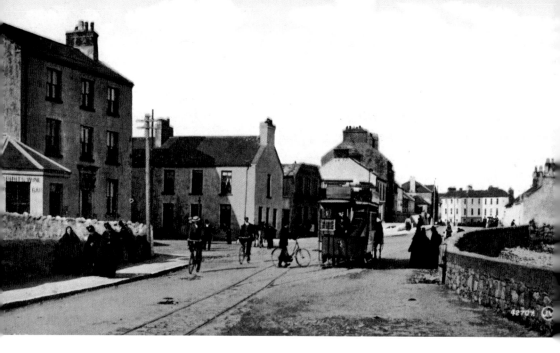

Salthill, *c.* 1904
The Galway to Salthill tramway service opened in 1879, linking its Foster Street depot to its terminus in front of the Eglinton Hotel via Eyre Square, Shop Street, Mainguard Street, Dominick Street, Sea Road, the Crescent and Lower Salthill. Its terminus at Salthill was the most westerly tramway terminus in Europe.

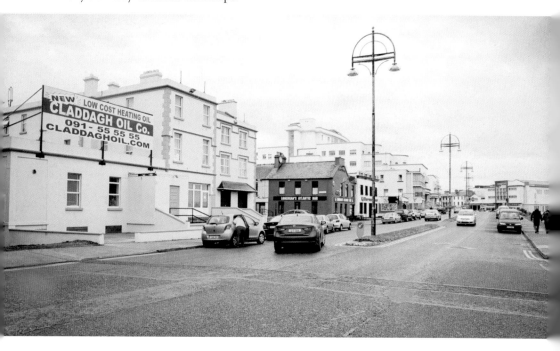

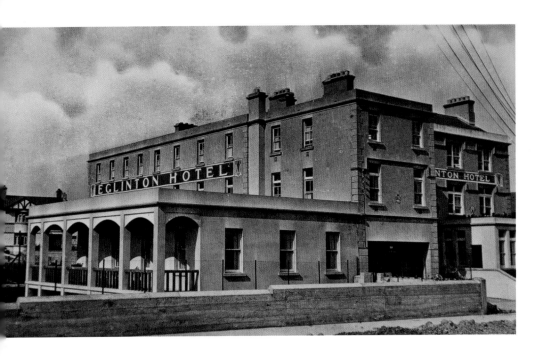

The Eglinton Hotel, Salthill, 1940s

The Eglinton Hotel opened in 1860 and became an instant landmark. It was named after Lord Eglinton (Lord Lieutenant of Ireland in 1852 and again from 1858 and 1859), who gave his consent in a letter dated 16 June 1860: 'Sir, I can have no objection to your new Hotel bearing my name, and I trust that the growing prosperity of Galway will render your investment a profitable one.' Several other developments in Galway were named in his honour, including the Eglinton Canal, opened by the Lord Lieutenant in 1852, and Eglinton Street. The hotel today functions as an asylum seekers' accommodation centre.

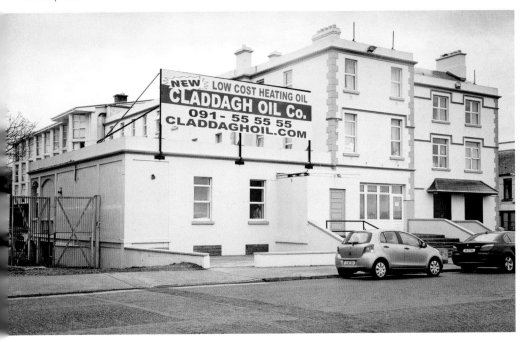

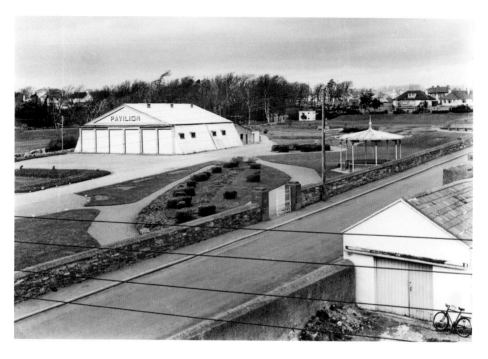

The Hangar, Salthill Park, c. 1960

In 1924 Galway Urban Council bought a disused aeroplane hangar and erected it in Salthill Park as a dancehall. Although officially called the Pavilion, it became more commonly known as the 'Hangar'. For a period it was managed by the Salthill Development Committee, with the profits being used for improvements in the vicinity. The venue played host to several notable international performers, including Jim Reeves and Johnny Cash, as well as home-grown talent such as Horslips, Planxty, Thin Lizzy and Rory Gallagher. It continued in use until the early 1970s when the Leisureland complex opened adjacently.

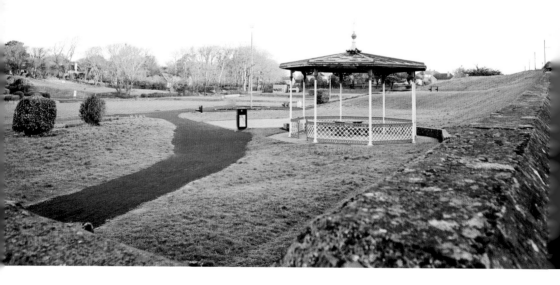

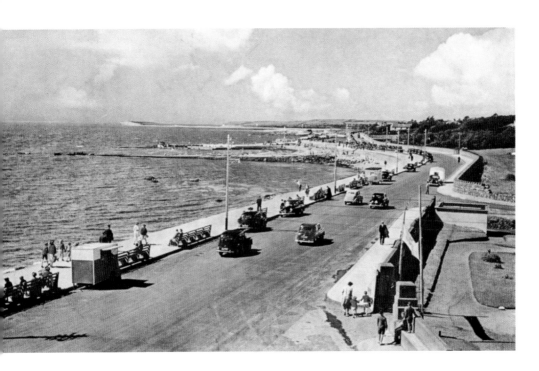

The Prom, Salthill, 1950s

A favourite Galway pastime is walking the 'Prom', a 2½-kilometre walkway stretching from the Claddagh to Blackrock along the shores of Galway Bay. It consists of three sections: Grattan Road, Seapoint Promenade and Salthill Promenade. In the early 1850s a Mr Barton, who had acquired a large tract of land between Salthill village and Blackrock, had a sea wall constructed to make the shoreline more suitable for bathing. Grattan Road promenade, built in the 1860s, connected the Claddagh and Salthill. It also acted as a sea wall preventing tidal flooding, which previously extended as far the bottom of Taylor's Hill.

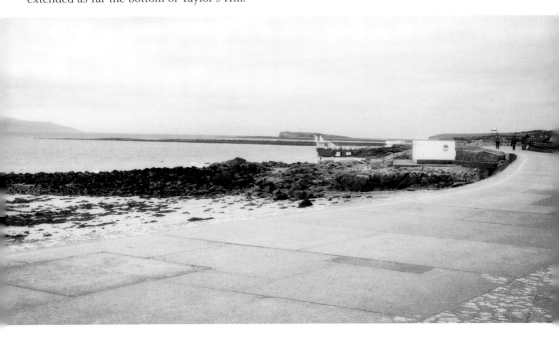

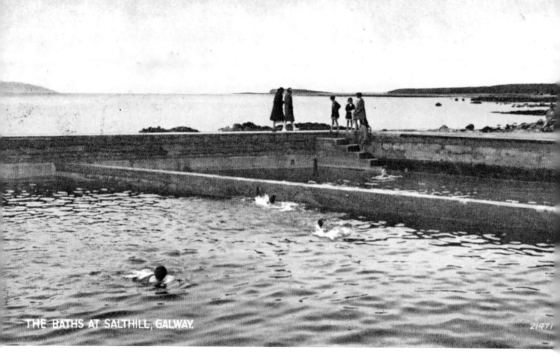

THE BATHS AT SALTHILL, GALWAY.

21471

Baths at Salthill, c. 1931

Bishop Browne of Galway, who served from 1937 onwards and wielded significant power locally, was very much against 'mixed bathing' at Salthill. In 1959 the Bishop declared that it was 'very wrong for unmarried couples to go bathing together. It is the cause of grave sins which bring shame and dishonour.' He used his influence to have a 'men only' sign put up at Blackrock. The beach and diving board remained the preserve of men until the early 1970s. The nearby beach known as Ladies Beach, opposite the Galway Bay Hotel, was for women and families.

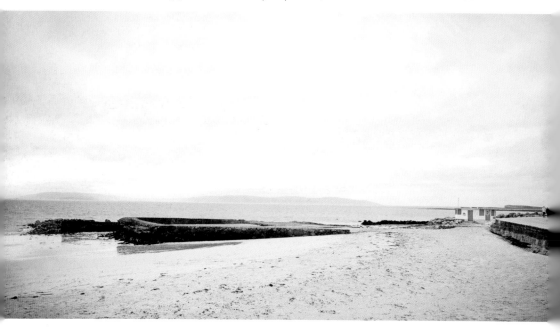

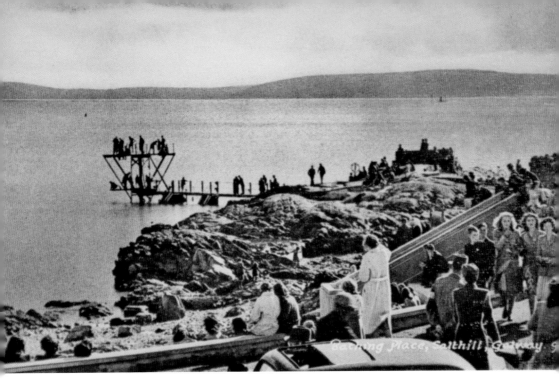

Blackrock Diving Tower, Salthill, 1930s

In the 1880s the first diving board was erected at Blackrock on the estate of Colonel O'Hara, much to his annoyance. In 1909 the landlord clashed with local residents over the issue of the board and access to the beach, inspiring one poet to pen the following lines: 'Oh! James astore / we all feel sore / after getting such a shock / When the Colonel roared / "take off that board / from my fine big Black Rock".' The diving tower, opened in 1954, was built at a cost of £5,500, of which £1,000 was contributed by the Salthill Citizen's Association.

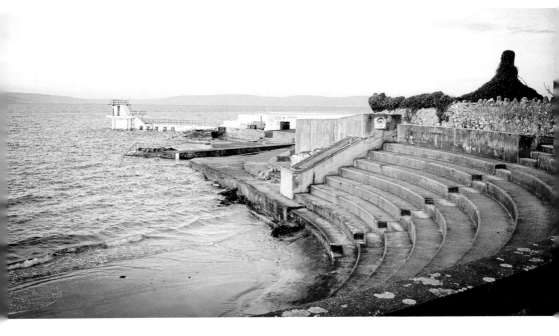

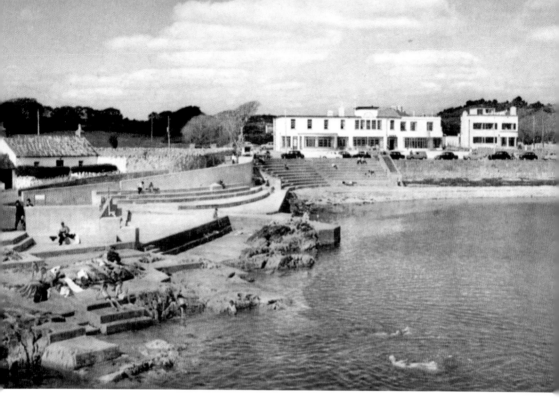

Blackrock, Salthill, *c.* 1960
According to tradition, Richard Gare Lynch, Mayor of Galway, fired a canon at a black rock in the bay when he was setting sail from Galway. The trip was such a success that in 1529 he decreed, 'all ships, with a Lynch in any of them that entered into the haven of Galway should shoot their great cannons at their passing by the black rock'. The practice was still being recorded in the early nineteenth century.

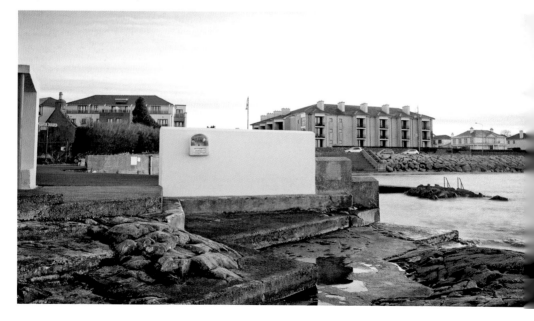

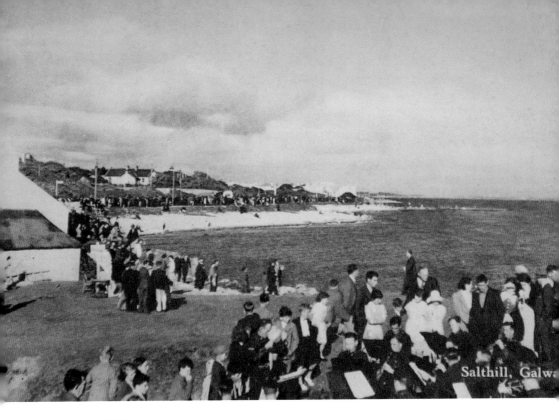

Galway Bay, Salthill, c. 1950
The song 'Galway Bay' was composed by Arthur Colahan: 'If you ever go across the sea to Ireland / Then maybe at the closing of your day / You will sit and watch the moon rise over Claddagh / And see the sun go down on Galway Bay'. It was popularised by Bing Crosby and featured in John Ford's cult classic *The Quiet Man* (1952), starring John Wayne and Maureen O'Hara.

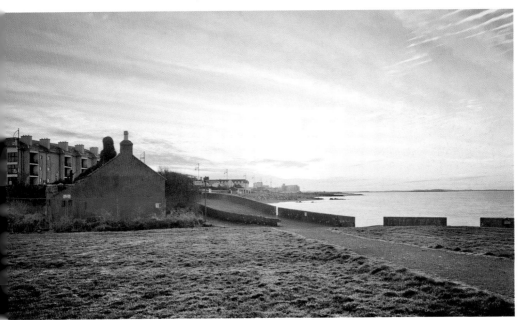

Acknowledgements

Thanks to my 'partner in crime', Tanya Williams, for her keen eye, photographic talents and boundless enthusiasm (regardless of the weather).

I would like to thank the following for their generosity in sharing their photographs and postcards: Glenn Dunne, National Library of Ireland; Dr Jim Higgins, Heritage Officer; Tom Kenny, Kenny's Bookshop; Anne Mooney (née Biddulph); Maureen Moran, Galway County Library; Colum O'Riordan, Irish Architectural Archive; Mick Quinn, Galway Civic Trust; Marja Van Kampen.

Finally, thanks to my 'partner in life and law', Vicky, for help assessing countless pairs of images. *Go raibh míle maith agaibh*!

Picture Credits: Derek Biddulph (pp. 19, 35, 36, 41, 44, 46, 51, 61 & 62); Claire Conroy (p. 12); Galway City Museum (pp. 13 & 14); Galway County Library (pp. 15, 16, 34, 71, 76, 85, 86, 89 & 93); Jim Higgins (pp. 18, 25, 49, 53, 63, 64, 67, 68, 70 & 79); Irish Architectural Archive (pp. 22, 38, 39, 40, 45, 50 & 52); John F. Kennedy Presidential Library & Museum (p. 84); Tom Kenny (p. 90); National Library of Ireland (pp. 2, 4, 5, 6, 8, 21, 24, 33, 48, 65, 74, 78 & 80); Marja Van Kampen (pp. 42, 43, 55, 58, 59, 60, 66 & 77).

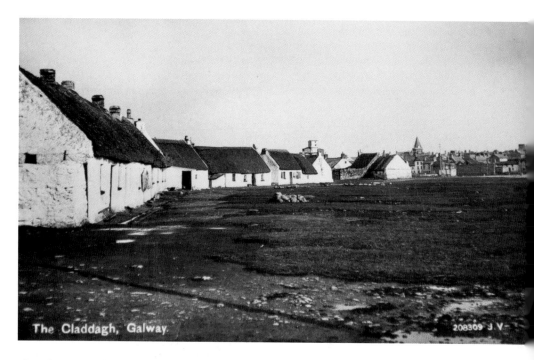

The Claddagh, Galway.

208309 J.V.

The Big Grass, Claddagh, c. 1929
In 1927 the Claddagh was deemed an 'unhealthy area' under the Housing of the Working Class Act 1890. On 29 November 1929 a compulsory purchase order was made and the majority were demolished by the mid-1930s.